CZECH DOCTOR
IN THE HEART
OF AFRICA

CZECH DOCTOR
IN THE HEART
OF AFRICA

Marcel Drlík, M.D.

AVENTINUM

Contents

To Albert, Goum, sister Christiane, father Marcello,
and all my black and white friends who have been
struggling to return hope to the sick in one of the
poorest parts of the world.

M.D.

Chapter One

Journey to the Heart of Africa

The plane shakes as it wildly speeds down the runway. One final wobble, and we rise steeply. Looking out of the window, I watch Prague International Airport slowly disappear in the darkness and clouds. Heavy raindrops roll down the windows. Only now do I begin to realize that I'll be able to return in one year at the earliest. I still can't believe that I've actually embarked on this mad adventure, having decided to leave for Central Africa as a medical doctor. See, I don't really know what I am going to do in Africa and I don't know much about the Central African Republic, or its inhabitants and their customs – only a few basic facts that I looked up on the Internet. What I had considered a while ago at the airport as the rational and right decision, now seems here, on this plane between heaven and earth, as sheer madness. Oh, what would I do if it all turned out to be a dream! I shivered when I realized it was too late to return.

It's pitch black beyond my small window. The Earth below has vanished for good. In the pleasant atmosphere of my surroundings, my memories revive little by little, rising up like living images, one by one.

It was one year ago, but it seems like only yesterday that I met father Anastasio, the prior of the Lady Victorious Church, by the Infant Jesus in Prague's Lesser Town. I wanted to learn something about the missionary activities of the Italian Carmelites in third world countries. That was soon after my first postgraduate diploma in surgery, and I had worked in the heart-surgery department of IKEM in Prague. I had already been toying for some time with the idea of applying my knowledge and experience to help people living in the poorest parts of the world.

The winter day that I met father Anastasio for the first time was gloomy like today. The walls of the Lesser Town Cloister were icy and it was bitterly cold in the church, but when I entered the sacristy I was welcomed by pleasant warmth. Father Anastasio was waiting for me. He knew why I came, and he immediately started talking with enthusiasm and vigor about the country where he had worked as a missionary for a number of years. It wasn't hard to see how much he had fallen in love with the African country and its people. At that moment, I thought it was just the thing I was looking for. "Do you think," I interrupted his interesting talk, "that a young doctor like me, with little clinical experience could be of any help in Africa?" "Of course," he smiled. "If you set out for Africa for some time, somebody can replace you in your work here, but nobody could stand in for you in Africa. There is a profound shortage of medical doctors there, and many of their hospitals are in such bad shape." So I made my decision. Anastasio welcomed my resolution with undisguised joy. He promised to cover the costs of my journey to Africa, and offered free accommodation and food at the mission where his brothers were working. In return I was happy to cure people in Africa for free, claiming no pay. "You might be able to work in the hospital of Bozoum, a town where Carmelites run a mission. But it is a state hospital, and I cannot promise the local authorities will agree to it. If not, you could work in one of the small dispensaries in Niem or Yolé that belong to the Church," Anastasio resumed kindly. "I don't speak a word of French and my English and Russian won't be of much help in the bush," I said, disenchanted. "That is not a problem," Anastasio shrugged it off, "If you want to, I can put you up in a boarding house run by Franciscan Sisters in Lyon, France. They run a mission in Bozoum, too. They will be happy to have you. Apart from a French course, you could undergo training in tropical medicine which you will surely need in Africa." This sounded both appealing and demanding. There seemed only one possible solution left. Without much hesitation I said yes.

My stay and studies in France helped me greatly, indeed, not only did I learn decent French, but I also completed a three-month training course in tropical medicine with a final exam at the Université Catholique de Lyon. Realizing I was to face problems other than that of my specialization in Africa, I arranged a practical at the pediatrics and child surgical wards of several Lyon hospitals. Most French doctors understood my situation. It was later that I learned some of them had actually spent some time in Africa. A variety of sponsors provided me with medical supplies and drugs. These were from France, Switzerland, Italy, and also from Prague. I shipped all the material with the help of the Italian Carmelites to The Central African Republic in advance. I also sent a request for a work permit to the local health ministry.

The intensive preparations for my one-year stay in Africa went smoothly beyond expectation. My first problems occurred shortly before my scheduled departure. I remember telephoning father Anastasio at least once a day, asking whether or not he had the promised visa for me. He always gave the same answer on the telephone: "See, dear Marcel, nothing has arrived yet, but it will, for sure." I admired Anastasio's optimism. I knew very well it was not easy to obtain a visa for the Central African Republic. This state has no diplomatic representation in my country, so all the negotiations with the local authorities in Bangui were mediated for a number of weeks solely by fax and telephone. I had to wait. Everything seemed hopeless even on Saturday morning, January 8, the day of my departure. The phone had been ringing from early morning and I kept answering it again and again to tell my friends who were calling to say goodbye, that I wasn't going anywhere because I didn't get the right papers. Anastasio even delayed his departure to Italy from Friday to Saturday at noon to help me with getting the visa in the morning. At 10 am, however, he had to leave for the airport. On his way, he handed me a few letters for his friends in African missions, and when we were saying goodbye, he assured me I would get my visa in four days at the latest. "I will still be in Italy by then," he thought, "but I guess you can manage."

After Anastasio left, no one expected any change in the situation. The stress and nervousness finally lifted around noon. While my mother was calmly preparing lunch, my brother and I, reconciled to my fate, launched into a game of chess. Then the telephone rang. I could recognize Anastasio's brother, the Indian priest Gerome, who had been answering the fax in Anastasio's absence to let me know if the visa had actually arrived. "Weeezah, maameh weeezah," Gerome rejoiced on the phone, he was so excited he could hardly speak Czech. This struck me. There were only a few hours left before my departure. The race against time began. I packed the things that were still lying around in my room into my suitcase and a rucksack, and double-checked my medical books and surgery equipment. My father and younger brother offered to bring my visa from the Carmelites, so that I could proceed with my final preparations for the journey. I then stashed away my passport and the coveted visa, and we left for the airport. Everything prior to my departure went so fast and in such a hurry, that none of us had time to think about either the coming long separation, or the danger of tropical diseases in equatorial Africa. There were none of the sad goodbyes that I had feared, but rather a cheerful farewell, full of peace and happiness that everything had actually worked out. Everyone wished me well.

The check-in went smoothly, with the exception of my rather bulky bag. I didn't want to let go of it, and when I tried to drag it along with me as a carry-on it created quite a stir. I can still see the officer giving me a stern look and asking me to open it after the x-ray check. He could hardly believe his eyes. His puzzled look darted over the paper box that was packed with my surgical instruments, and he made a curious expression. While he was nodding, all perplexed, I tried to explain what I needed all those scalpels for and why I had to have them with me in the plane. "If I lose those things in my bag, I will be of no use in Africa." "All right, go!" the officer finally said and swept his hand in resignation.

"Ladies and gentlemen, please fasten your seatbelts and put your seats into the upright position. In a few minutes we will be landing at Charles de Gaulle airport in Paris" the stewardess' pleasant voice interrupts my recollections. After a few minutes I am in the transit hall, I have never seen such a large airport before. There are crowds of passengers with bags, information screens flashing, and the sumptuous shops with luxurious goods are all glittering. "Where now?" I look around. I had been told in Prague International Airport that the plane from Paris to Bangui leaves from a different terminal than the one we landed in from Prague.

After a brief search I finally find a bus, and ride to the other terminal. The sky is overcast, dark, and it's raining. I only have to find the right gate, and as I look around inquisitively, I recognize a familiar face. There goes Angelo, the Italian dentist who has been working for years in the Yolé mission, which is about 100 miles from my future point of work. I know him. I once met him in Prague; father Anastasio introduced him to me. "Ciao, Angelo!" I shout and head towards him, dragging my weighty bag behind me. There is only a light bag over Angelo's shoulder. "I left all the rest in Africa," he explains. "I went back home to Italy only for a short holiday, just to breathe in some cold air," he laughs. When we enter the plane, I suddenly lose track of him. It was later I learned that he – 'the traveler of experience' – had snuck into the business class section for the fatiguing nine-hour flight, although though he only had economy class tickets like me.

When I enter the plane I realize that this won't be a comfy flight like the one from Prague to Paris. There are none of the calm polished businessmen with briefcases, but a throng of yelling people, struggling to squeeze their capacious baggage into the space above the seats. Some of them eventually give up and use, quite unscrupulously, the free room in the aisle. More and more people scurry over the baggage in the aisle, clumsily jumping over it, and stumbling. There are arguments and quarrels. Stewards try to keep order as they walk the grumbling passengers calmly to their reserved seats. Most of the travelers are African. A poised older man in a flowered shirt takes the seat next to mine. His face is sunburnt and full of wrinkles. He keeps making constant demands for an aspirin during the flight. He tells me he is Portuguese and that he is a forest keeper in the southern parts of the land, on the Zaire border. "And where are you heading?" he asks with interest. "To work in the Bozoum hospital." "Well, good luck," he grins. "Only wood works in Africa, not the natives, for sure." I don't feel like talking anymore, it's long past midnight and I want to get some sleep before dawn.

A nervous running of stewards and excited voices wake me up about half past one. I turn my head and see an old African woman who is vomiting and falling into a state of oblivion. "I am

"That's Oubangui, and there is Congo on the other bank. See
the vast rainforest?" says my knowledgeable Portuguese neighbor.

not even in Africa yet, and my work starts," it occurs to me. Oh
well. I rise from my seat to tell the crew I'm a doctor. They are
relieved, apparently, as they were at a loss before. The Sahara is
below us already, and that means hours and hours without the
possibility of landing. The captain actually asks me whether he
should turn around and land at the nearest airport. I try to calm
the members of the crew. I assure them that the state of the
African woman I had just examined is not too serious, and that
they can carry on flying. On the captain's request, I record an
account of this event into the logbook and then I go back to
sleep.

It is early morning. The Sun has not yet made it to the
horizon. Our plane lands in N'Djamena in Chad. Everything

seems so peculiar, so not European. The airport is enclosed in by an infinite and desolate, sunburst-colored steppe, threaded with pools and dead branches from the marshland of nearby Chad Lake. The landscape here seems so bleak and desolate! I am glad when we proceed with our flight immediately after refueling. Right after takeoff I take advantage of my friendly relations with the crew and the captain allows me to watch the African sunrise. It sure is a fantastic experience! The plane continues to head south as I watch the red ball rapidly ascending. Then suddenly the clouds part underneath us and we are descending again. I can see small houses on the ground and little fields peeping out of rich greenery. There is a wide river on the right. "That's Oubangui, and there is Congo on the other bank. See the vast rainforest?" says my knowledgeable Portuguese neighbor. The onboard radio interrupts him. "Dear passengers, we have just landed in Bangui, the capital of the Central African Republic. Please take notice it is forbidden to photograph the airport, police stations, office and administrative buildings, and state boarder lines. Trespassers will be prosecuted." I was actually looking forward to taking a few pictures, but now the only option was to bury the camera in my bag. The plane stops, and the doors open with a hiss.

So here I am. The M'Poko Airport is the only international airport in the Central African Republic. It consists of a single dilapidated, one-story building. There is a fortified military base right next to it.

The temperature difference between Prague and Bangui, now in January, is about 86°F. My flannel shirt awkwardly sticks to my body, and the first beads of sweat roll down my forehead. "Hope I get used to this," I wonder as I start descending the stairs with my crammed backpack. Whoever expected a bus to drive the passengers with their luggage to the airport hall was simply wrong. So we all take our bags and proceed through the area to the customs and passport control. As I walk past the huge wheels of the landing gear, I can see the local porters just starting to unload the plane.

"Votre visa n'est pas valide – Your visa is invalid," I am told by the stone-faced local policeman. He confiscates my passport with the coveted visa before I manage to object. In vain I try to protest and argue. "Get your luggage first and then go to that counter," he remarks with annoyance and turns to another passenger. I gloomily walk to the moving belt and see the bumpy outline of the first piece of luggage. I anxiously await the appearance of my own suitcase, in vain. There is no luggage left, everything is gone. I stand like a statue, and watch the empty belt as it noisily slides past. I feel dumbfounded. "Well, that's a fair beginning here," I tell myself, angrily thinking that I am near the equator without my passport, my visa, my papers, my suitcase is gone and I'm wearing winter clothes. "Thank God I brought my books and surgery tools with me." When I look at my backpack, I feel grateful to the Prague officer. Almost desperately I think of Anastasio waving me goodbye. "Be prepared, you will have problems," he said. "What kind?" I was curious. "Well, I don't know, but there will be plenty of them. There is always trouble in Africa." I didn't fully understand him then, but I'm beginning to now.

As I stood there pondering, Angelo approaches, along with father Saverio, and Enrico, the carpenter, who came to pick us up from the airport. Saverio and Enrico are cheerful, thirty-five year old Italians. They are all shaggy and sandy from red dust. "Welcome! Welcome!" they holler. I try to explain my troubles. "Well, that may be unpleasant, but it is quite usual," Saverio isn't surprised at all. Thanks to a small bribe, I am allowed to leave the airport and go to the city. There isn't much we can do about the whole situation, anyway. It's Sunday and all the offices are closed.

Soon we get into a Toyota jeep, and head to the Centre d'accueil – the mission boarding house for newcomers. From the airport to the city, there is a wide asphalt road full of holes. There are plank stands and clay shacks on both sides. Just like all the other cars, we adroitly snake through crowds of people. Here and there I can see a man pushing a cart overstuffed with various goods. Some timber merchants even fasten a few twenty-foot long trunks onto such a vehicle, dragging them for a few miles. Rhythmical African beats come from all corners of this incredible human mass. We pass parliament and the Arc de Triumph. These mighty buildings contrast with the poor shacks all around. The whole city sinks in clouds of red dust, which settles on everything, everywhere. It covers plants, trees, corrugated iron and hay on the roofs. It uncompromisingly penetrates our car and it creaks in between our teeth. The sky is amazingly blue and the dust tinges the daylight with a pink hue. And the trees! They are so huge and they have wide roots rising three feet above ground, which look like the fins of some gigantic fish. It is a completely different world.

In a few minutes we pull up at the Centre d'accueil, right next to the Notre Dame Cathedral. It's a square shaped complex of buildings with a small yard. Dusty off-road cars of various makes and ages park there underneath the huge trees. The whole ground is fenced and guarded. The site belongs to the archdiocese. It serves as a transfer station for all the missionaries both coming from Europe into the African bush, and returning back to Europe. For a decent sum of money one can sleep, eat, make a phone call or send a fax from here. A telephone is a real rarity here, and most missions lack the luxury.

After a short welcome with the permanent residents of the site, I get the keys to my room. I enter the door right from the yard, as if I were in a motel. The furnishings are plain: a table, a chair, a bed with a mosquito net, and a washstand.

I would like to take a closer look at the site, but I don't have much time. It's Sunday and the celebratory mass begins in a short while. In a distance I hear native drums and temperamental singing of the locals. All in sweat, I lay down my thirty-pound backpack, and wipe the sweat off of my face with a sigh. Am I ever to see my suitcase again?

It's only about 200 yards to the cathedral, but I am not even half way through and the heat of the sun at noon is already commencing to mercilessly scorch my head. I am angry with myself and I promise myself never to go out under the sun without cover again.

The size of the building surprises me. It is a spacious, but relatively low building, built of bare red brick. The roof is covered by corrugated iron. There is a low, square, open-roofed tower on each side of the entrance. When I enter, I pay close attention to the cathedral windows. They are not glazed, but merely vertically divided by planks. They look something like vents, and function as such, providing ventilation as well as shade for the interior.

There are loads of people jammed in the cathedral already. I cannot see a single white. The Africans are evidently part of the city's upper classes. Men wear diligently ironed shirts, women wear long, multicolored dresses and cute little hats set on elaborate hairdos. Looking around, I can see some kind of bat flying above people's heads. When it flies nearer, I discern a huge, beautiful butterfly, eight inches wide. I have never seen anything like this before. The celebratory mass runs in a joyous atmosphere. The Africans are fond of lengthy singing parts, swinging and clapping in rhythm – the Sunday Mass thus gets quite long, keeping in mind European standards. Eventually, being utterly exhausted by heat, weariness and all the various new impressions during the several-hour-long celebration, I return back to the Centre d'accueil. Of all things, I hunger for substantial sleep the most.

I wake up late in the afternoon. The sleep has uplifted me. Since I know the mosquitoes will be swarming after dark, I check my mosquito net. I actually find a few holes in it, and fix them with the help of some little strings taken from the Christmas sweets I had removed from our tree before I left. I have not slept in a tropical region before, and I've read quite a lot about malaria and I have to confess I have a few concerns. Getting sick right at the beginning of my stay might not be the best thing to do.

Night falls at six o'clock. I take a short walk to the cathedral before dinner, but then I return quickly. I don't feel quite secure in the dark, strange city. The Moon comes out. It seems rather strange at first. Its shape is like the Turkish half moon; both of its ends are turned upwards, as if a large letter "U" was shining in the sky.

Chapter Two

In the African Bush

"Lève-toi – get up!" Saverio, the young Carmelite, is knocking at my door. "We are going to go look for your visa and suitcase," he urges me. All others, including my co-traveler Angelo, have already left for the bush. Only Saverio has stayed to help me deal with the authorities. Apparently, he is not very happy about this unplanned, prolonged stay in hot and humid Bangui. "We must settle this as soon as possible," he says with determination. Unfortunately, we are to be dogged by luck. All I get at the police station is a tiny piece of paper with a round stamp on it, they call it "confirmation of a temporary confiscation of passport" – I have to make do with this until the problem is solved. We don't make any progress at the Air France office either. They still don't know anything about my lost suitcase. Moreover, the African clerk is teasing me: "You say you lost your clothes? But you have clothes on you! And you're dressed so nicely! So what's the matter?" Saverio sighs: "You are in Africa, my boy, and there is no hurry here. We have to just be patient, and go bother the clerks again tomorrow. It's a matter of whoever loses patience first, although them Africans have heaps of it."

In two days I finally get news of my suitcase. It had gone to Benin instead of the Central African Republic, and in four days it reaches Bangui. Its not even ransacked! I can't even believe it. Fortune has smiled on me. I have summer clothes, finally! My joy isn't to last too long, however. It all vanishes when I begin to inquire into the fate of my work request I sent with all my documentation from Prague to Africa four months ago. Alarmed, I realize the papers haven't made it to the Ministry of Heath in the Capital, and are allegedly stuck in N'Ganuday, a small border town almost 400 miles from here, at some white doctor's who is in charge of processing my work permit.

The fourth day we are left with the same answer from the police: "Your passport has not been processed by the computer yet." Well, I don't know what kind of computer they work with, if the mere entry of the name and passport number has swallowed a number of days. Our protests don't make things easier, and nobody takes them into account. Saverio evidently loses patience. "You won't need your passport in the bush, when someone from the mission gets here in a few weeks, he can pick it up for you on his way. In the meantime, you can spend some time in Niem, at the dispensary of father Tiziano. You will at least get familiar with Africa and learn some of the local vernacular." I readily accept. By now I have with me the most important thing – my suitcase, and frankly, I am getting rather tired of the noisy and dirty Bangui. Moreover, I can't wait to start working somewhere.

It's almost noon. "If we want to reach Baoro today, we must leave soon," Saverio decides. I quickly put my luggage in the back of the little truck; he empties the letterbox of the latest mail for Baoro. The country's local post doesn't operate, thus forcing the missions to develop their own delivery system from the capital. The employees of the transfer station pick up the coming mail regularly at the airport; then they sort it out into boxes for the individual missions. After that someone arrives from one of the missions and empties the postbox.

We finally leave. With difficulty we make our way through the inconceivably huge crowds in the street. From all sides I can hear the shrill voices of peddlers, running about and offering miscellaneous goods. Shabby cabs are honking, and jeeps full of soldiers are passing by every minute. There is a lot of dirt floating in the air and the midday heat is intolerable. Slowly we move to the edge of the city. There is an army camp. From a distance we can see a thick chain lying across the road and a camouflaged soldier with a Kalashnikov on his shoulder controlling the passing vehicles. We don't have any problems, thank god. The soldiers seem to be much more interested in the Arabian merchants driving big trucks packed with a variety of goods than in our car with the "Mission Catholique" lettering.

We keep driving north. There is a thin asphalt road that goes all the way to M'Bossembélé. It's still almost 200 miles from here. I learned there are only about 250 miles of asphalt road in the country, so I guess now I have the chance to get to know almost all of it in a single day. All the other roads are earthen. African bush… I feel like I'm dreaming.

I can finally see with my own eyes the landscape I had known only from travel brochures before. There are just bushes, and tall grass; sometimes we drive through small villages full of low earthen shacks with straw roofs, only to be followed by more grass and bush land. Every once in a while I can see stripes of smoke rising up slowly in the sky. Fires are not uncommon during the dry season.

I suddenly realize that Saverio has been sullen for more than half an hour. His eyes are glued to the needle of the fuel indicator. It has dropped into the red section. "In all this hurry, I forgot to fill the tank", he says quietly." The nearest petrol station is all the way up in M'Bossembélé. I hope we make it. We are short of water too…" He stops, allowing me to think through the implications. We are all alone on the road. We haven't met a car for more than an hour. The situation looks desperate. The needle of the fuel indicator has been pointing to zero for some time already. We hope the engine will keep on running. The both of us are quiet and anguished with a sole thought occupying our minds: "Gas station, we must make it to the gas station." Eventually, and miraculously perhaps, we drive into M'Bossembélé, unspeakably relieved, with the last few drops of gas in the tank almost entirely depleted. We pull up at the gas station, fill the tank and – for a song – buy some gorgeous bananas from a few kids. Saverio, however, declares with a worried look: "We set off too late, and it is a long way to Baoro still. By the time we reach the end of the road, night will fall. Then we'll be forced to proceed very slowly and cautiously to avert any potholes. It's going to be a long, difficult journey."

We have been drudging along on the earthen path for about two hours already. It's pitch black beyond the car windows. We can hear cicadas, and – unfamiliar for me – night bird cries. Saverio keeps changing course every minute to avoid the craters in the path. Then he rapidly stops. We both jump forward. The car lowers and then jumps up again. My head hits the roof and, shocked, I glance at Saverio. "I saw the pothole at the very last moment," he utters apologetically, and starts up the Toyota again. Our lights are on, but it's virtually impossible to see ahead, as if a thick fog went down on the bushland. "There must be a truck ahead of us," Saverio explains. "The dust then sticks in the air, making it impossible to see anything. We have to overtake it. The truck drivers prefer driving at night to avoid the heat. They steer all the way to Duala, to the sea. We are on the Trans-African road here, mind you." It's hard for me to grasp: then is this 14-feet-wide earthen path, full of holes and cracks, the celebrated thousand mile long road linking the western and the eastern African coasts?

Two jolting tiny red lights suddenly pop up in the darkness. "Hold on, and watch out!" Saverio shouts and starts honking like mad, drawing near the rear of the mighty truck, with its trailer

It is later – in the Bozoum Hospital while dealing with various traffic accidents – that I fully realize the great danger of local driving.

and container in tow. At first, the driver does not mind us at all, and then, perhaps a little tired of us, he veers slightly to the right. In the dusty cloud we can only sense the position of the truck by its taillights. Saverio sharply turns the steering wheel, and steps on the gas. Our car is rubbing against a wall of tall grass on the left, and bush twigs are whipping our windows. Ahead of the truck, eventually! We are both relieved. It is later – in the Bozoum Hospital while dealing with various traffic accidents – that I fully realize the great danger of local driving, even when there is very little traffic here. The roads are in dreadful shape, the cars are in worse, and the truck drivers especially are famous for their recklessness. The survival of the fittest, I guess.

"We've made it! Finally!" Saverio cries with relief, and points ahead. There is a grouping of lights, shimmering in the darkness.

"Those are the fires of Baoro," he explains. Slowly we drive into the city. Many people are walking down the road, and there are lots of small shops, lit by kerosene lamps. We pass the "point rond", the main intersection, and then we pull up at the mission gate. The mission consists of a small church and a set of buildings surrounded by a fence.

Saverio leads me to the refectory, where he introduces me to father Robert. "Welcome here!" says the superior of the mission, and shakes my hand. "You may grab some food in the kitchen, take a wash in the bathroom, and – yes – let me show you your room. The furnishings are simple, yet clean and practical." I am taken by this pleasant surprise – I didn't expect such a thing in the bush. "And don't worry about your mosquito net, there aren't any mosquitoes here," cries father Roberto after me, taking leave.

While drifting into sleep, I really appreciate how well one can breathe here. The air isn't too humid, and it's much cooler than in Bangui, just like back home in summer. It is later that I learn the missionaries regard the Baoro mission – by virtue of its furnishings and excellent climate conditions – as a "sanatorium".

Chapter Three

Baoro

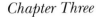

The next day, at breakfast, I meet father Marcello. He is a fifty-year-old Italian, with a big smile and white hair. He came for me from Bozoum where he has been working for eighteen years already. "We shall leave after lunch. It's only about 150 miles from here," he remarks kindly. And he adds, still smiling: "Everyone is looking forward to meeting you. I can't wait to introduce you at our mission. You are expected at the hospital, too. But I guess it wouldn't do much good for you if you started working straight ahead. You should find your bearings in Africa first, and learn some Sango. The nurses at the hospital speak French, but the patients are simple people from the village – they speak the local language only. And, moreover, you haven't got your work permit from the ministry yet. You should go to Niem after the weekend; it's a small village near the border of Cameroon. Father Tiziano has a small walk-in ward there. He is a doctor, like you, and might teach you a few useful things." I nod.

I have the whole morning to myself. I've heard the sisters from the mission have recently opened a small clinic here. I go and check it out right after breakfast. The first patients are restlessly pacing in front of a small, low, concrete house. It's early morning: I encounter only an African assistant there. Curiously I look around the small room. A table, some chairs, a cabinet with carefully arranged essential medicaments, and an examination bed. The equipment is more than modest. When the man finds out I am a doctor, he starts letting in the first patients, taking no reserve. I try to stop this ardent activity of his, but to no avail. There comes a woman with a small child. While the little kid does not look ill at all and keeps staring at me curiously, his mother gestures emotionally and pours a stream of incomprehensible words at me. She tries to hand me a dirty plastic bag. I don't understand a thing. I look vacantly and helplessly. The assistant, thank god, saves the situation as he pulls an inch long white worm out of the bag. "She discovered it in the child's stool in the morning," he translates from Sango, as he points at the woman with his chin. I take a look at the unattractive contents of the bag. I remember seeing a sketch of something similar in my parasitology textbook a few years ago. "This is a special, smaller type of tapeworm," I say in a convincing tone. "A microscope will help to find out whether or not there are pupae in the stools, and we can use an atlas to specify the class." "I'll take care of it," the assistant rejoices. "So here you are!" I hear an amiable woman's voice behind me. I turn my head and see a sister who has just arrived from the mission. "So, how do you like our infirmary?" she adds with a smile. I am really happy that she freed me, so I speak really highly of everything. "Take a glimpse at our school," she suggests in a friendly way. I nod and say goodbye to both of them.

The school is behind the mission, at the end of the village. The small house is shaded with mango trees. I furtively peep in from the entrance, but I can't escape the attention of the little African children. Suddenly all the little black heads turn to the

"Take a glimpse at our school," my colleague suggests in a friendly way.

spot where I stand motionless. "Come in!" the teacher, a nun, gives me a nod. "Say hello, children!" The tots rise up and they recite in a well-mannered way: "Bon-djoor Mah-sehr." I guess that they've said: "Bon jour, Marcel." How come they know my name? I am really baffled. "Oh no, they don't know your name, the thing is you didn't hear well," the teacher explains. "They said ‚Bon jour ma soeur!' meaning ‚Good morning, sister!' This is all they know in French. We teach the first graders in the local tongue, but when a visitor appears, they like to show off with their 'French'". I don't mind at all that they called me "nun" and I greet them in return. They reward me with twenty cute smiles.

I'm sorry to leave, but I must make it for lunch, before I hit the road again.

The nuns visit me after the meal. "The calendar says your name day is in a few days, Marcel. Here's something from us." They give me a small box of Turkish honey from Italy. It's clear that such a thing is very precious in the bush. To buy it is impossible: one can only bring it from Europe. I refuse, embarrassed, but I am surprised by their candid reply. "Of course it is a precious thing. But we don't really think you are going to eat it. When you meet someone, and you want to cheer him, then give it to him. He may then pass the honey box to someone else." I can hardly believe my ears; the nuns are absolutely serious, however. I was used to supermarkets with loaded stands, flowing over with similar sorts of candy and sweets: this is for me, again, an encounter with the African reality. I never dared to eat the honey. In a few months, I would give it as a birthday present to a nun in Bozoum.

Chapter Four

In Bozoum At Last

In the afternoon, father Marcello and I depart from Baoro, and undertake the journey to Bozoum. I am finally going to see – eight days have passed since my arrival – my future place of work! Marcello is at home on the road. He deftly avoids the potholes and maintains a speed of 50 mph. He doesn't use the air-conditioning, trying to save expensive fuel. In order to avoid death from the heat, we keep the car windows open, swallowing pounds of dust in the process.

"That's impossible! Can you see?" Marcello gives a surprised cry and focusing, points ahead with his finger. There are two huge black, tailless monkeys crossing our path. "I've been here for eighteen years, but I have never seen gorillas here in the savannah. They live about 200 miles south of here. Maybe hunters are going after them. "Except for a few eagles and herons, we haven't spotted any other animals on the way. As the Sun begins to sink below the horizon, the landscape suddenly changes. Small mounds slowly appear in the bush, which has been until now as flat as a table.

"We are at home," Marcello rejoices, his face glowing with happiness. I didn't really understand his enthusiasm then, but later, as I was returning from my frequent trips back to Bozoum, I would always remember this and experience joy similar to his. Yes, the Bozoum mission was a place in the vast African plains where I would come back to take a rest, where I would safely lie down under my mosquito net, and drink my filtered water, having thus no fear from parasites; where I could talk to kind people and gather my strength again. The place became my second home and I always felt happy and well there.

Except for a German married couple from the humanitarian organization DROP, who live at the other end of Bozoum, the missionaries and the people working in the mission are the only whites in town. The entire Central African countryside faces a similar kind of situation. The last white traders took leave after the withdrawal of the French soldiers. There is no tourism in the Central African Republic. The insufficiency, and poor shape of the roads, the remoteness, and the lack of adequate security of the country are to blame. There are no tourists, and that's why every white face attracts a lot of attention.

We drive through the town at night. I can't see much, just some small fireplaces in front of various houses, or kerosene lamps on stands and the shining eyes of the natives. We leave the town, turn left, and through a grove drive up to a small hill. Two lit lamps mark the gateway to the mission. I can see figures sitting on the veranda; hurriedly they come to greet us. "That's great you've got electricity here," I tell Marcello. "Yes, there is a gas generator in the mission, running from dusk to half past nine. It makes the day last a little longer. Here at the equator, the Sun rises and sets, every day, regularly, at six."

Tired we get out of the car to meet some members of the mission: father Norberto with his patriarchal gray beard, who runs all the mission schools in the bush, Sebastian – a young Indian priest, and Francesca – an Italian girl, who came here as a volunteer for one year. She takes care of the children in the kindergarten and lives next door with the Franciscan Sisters. I'll meet the Sisters tomorrow, as it's already too late today.

Everyone in the mission has had his or her dinner so father Marcello and I eat the leftovers. The menu is simple: pasta with tomato sauce and lettuce salad. "Did you get this at the market?" I point with my finger at the green leaves of salad.

"Oh no," Marcello says shaking his head. "There is a small garden behind the kitchen with mangos, grapefruits, papayas, and even some banana trees. You can take a look at them tomorrow, if you feel like, but don't go there now." "Why?" I wonder. "Did you bring a flashlight with you?" Marcello asks, granting no answer for my previous request. "Of course," I nod in agreement.

"Well, that's good," the Carmelite looks contented. "After we switch off the lights at half past nine, you mustn't take a single step without a flashlight, and especially not in the orchard at the back of our mission: there are quite a few snake holes back there. Snakes are night animals, at dusk they creep out and hunt for insects.

Trust me, you wouldn't enjoy it if you bumped into one. You should watch out during the day as well. Mind your step!" I am taken aback. "Are there any extremely poisonous kinds here, too?" "All of them are," Marcello smiles indulgently as he turns his head to Gerome, an African cook around thirty-five, who is now cleaning the table. "Taah teneh – That's right" Gerome joins in our conversation, "but did you imagine snakes live only on the ground? Well, if you see a leaf fall, when there is no wind, you better avoid that leaf. Those green tree snakes are particularly dangerous." I am no specialist in ophidians, but I am acquainted with a few poisonous sorts.

"Cobra i Mamba yeke? – Do cobra and mamba live here?" for the first time, I decided to employ some of the words in the vernacular I had learned on my way here. The black guy gives me a big smile: I can see the two rows of snowy white teeth. He seems happy to hear a "new" white man speaking his mother tongue. "A yeke mingih – there's plenty of them," I can hear as he moves away from the table with the dishes.

"Is there antiserum at the mission?"

"No, there's none. Anyway, it lasts only for a short time and it has to be stored in a cool place."

"And at the hospital?"

"Oh no, by no means. The only thing the Africans use is ‚pierre noire' – ‚the black stone', a substance made of carbonized cow's bones. It has a very high absorbing potential, and the ability to sop up blood and poison from a fresh wound."

"This can prevent poisoning?"

"Sometimes it might," Marcello admits timidly.

Unfortunately – as I found out later in the hospital – the black stone isn't really effective. Snakes represent constant danger for all the inhabitants of Bozoum, both African and European. After such an encouraging dialogue I go and pull out the flashlight from my suitcase.

Once I manage to rinse off the layers of red dust, I begin to carry the luggage from the car into my room. On a termite-resistant concrete floor, there is a plain wooden table, chair, closet, and a bed. On the white wall, there is a crucifix of dark brown wood, and an ancient petroleum lamp underneath it. Hastily, before the lights are switched off, I unpack my suitcase. I double-check my mosquito net, and take a look underneath the bed and behind the closet.

I bend down under the table and then I block the space under the door. I don't want to be surprised by any poisonous spiders, scorpions or snakes!

It's terribly hot inside the mosquito net. From outside I can hear drum beats, chirping cicadas, and the rustling of bat's wings underneath the roof. I don't fall asleep for a long time, but I am happy. I am finally 'at home'.

Chapter Five

My First Impressions

In the morning they tell me the African doctor will be in the hospital for the most part today, and that he awaits me in the afternoon. That's lucky, since he is usually away on a business trip. He isn't involved only in this hospital: as most African country doctors he is actually the hospital's director, i.e. he is in charge of providing the supplies, filling in the papers, and attending various meetings about health policies. Not only that, as the prefect chief of health, he is in charge of the three other sub-prefecture hospitals in Paua, N'Ganuday and Boccaranga. The prefecture covers an area equal to three quarters of the Czech Republic. Unfortunately, there is no other doctor in the Bozoum hospital. I still have some time to look around the new surroundings before my scheduled meeting.

Bozoum is the capital of the Ouham-Pendé prefecture: an administrative unit parallel to the Czech "kraj" or district. It lies

The town consists of small one-story houses, scattered on both banks of a small river.

on the northwestern edge of the Central African Republic. It has about 17 thousand inhabitants and stretches across a valley between two hills, which likely belong to the Karré range. Rather than a mountain range, however, it is a series of small hills rising from a plain covered with bush and scrub. Although the landscape gives the impression of lowland, it is actually a plateau, rising about 2600 feet above sea level. The climate here is thus dryer and cooler than in Bangui.

The town consists of small one-story houses, scattered on both banks of a rivulet that diffuses into the marsh, which is overgrown with rushes. Thanks to the local geography there is never a shortage of mosquitoes and malaria in Bozoum.

On various places I saw the natives making the earthen bricks most small houses are built of. It is only dry grass, however, they

On various places I saw the natives making the earthen bricks most small houses are built of.

use as material for their roofs. Unfortunately, the lifespan of these huts is very short. In a few years they succumb to the termites that slowly keep digging small tunnels in the walls all the way up to the roof, which they eventually consume. Every two years it becomes necessary to change the dry grass, and every once in a while to build a new house. The use of cement or molded bricks offers a solution: this is, however, financially unattainable for most of the people. The only lasting houses in town are the town hall, hospital, police station, mission, and a few houses belonging to well-to-do merchants or officers.

All houses literally disappear in the rich greenery of the mango and papaya trees. Africans are very fond of them and find them beneficial, planting them near their homes. No such trees grow freely in the bush.

Small shops – owned chiefly by Arabian traders – line both sides of the main street in Bozoum. It is actually the only street in town lit by streetlamps. It was in January that I would see groups of teenagers sitting around every lamp: they would make use of

They lift water out of the few functioning, usually self-dug, wells.

the dim light to study and read. Unfortunately, this public light survived only until February, when the generator ran out of gas, after which Bozoum was covered in darkness.

The town has a very simplistic water supply. Although the yearly fees are low, very few inhabitants use it. Except for the hospital and the households of wealthier Arabian traders, most Africans don't recognize why they should they pay for water, so they continue to bring unwholesome water from the river, or they lift water out of the few functioning, usually self-dug, wells.

The marketplace is the heart of the town. Lots of people show up every morning. On concrete tables or directly on the ground, business is flourishing. Here you can buy bananas, manioc, corn, meat, spices, but also roasted ants, bats, snakes or smoked

The marketplace is the heart of the town. Lots of people show up every morning.

caterpillar, imported from the rainforests in the south. The Arabian merchants usually sell the natives clothes, textiles, shoes, mats, cigarettes, beer, and even Coca-Cola, which seems to be everywhere in the World. When the locals want something of a different kind, they usually have to undertake a trip to the capital city. The Central African Republic has no industry of its own and relies on imported goods for its various needs. Such goods are then, of course, very expensive and hard to obtain.

Chapter Six

The Hospital

I set out for the hospital in the afternoon. I don't have to go far. It stands on a small hill in the vicinity of the mission. As I am slowly rising up the dusty road, I ponder how my first encounter with the local doctor will turn out. Soon I pass by a few small houses, which are already a part of the hospital. The hospital itself consists of a complex of six low brick houses. Inside, there are wards for pediatrics, surgery, internal medicine, an infirmary, and a small pharmacy. The buildings embrace a circular yard with huge, ancient mango trees. I can feel the penetrating stares from numerous pairs of eyes of people who camp there, in the shade of the mighty umbrageous trees. In most cases these are the patients' relatives: they prepare food, bathe their sick and convalescing family members and also wash the clothes and used bandages. They simply take care of their sick. This is important because the hospital provides no such care. Suddenly, I must stop. Here comes a herd of goats! How did they make it here? As I am staring at them, I glimpse a group of small hogs quietly grazing in front of the house labeled "surgical ward". Then, I frighten away hens from the house labeled "Maternité", i.e. maternity ward. I can't help but wonder. All of the city animals feel free to come here to graze. There isn't any fencing!

It shouldn't be too difficult to find the doctor's office, but where should I begin? I venture to knock at the door. In a moment, there comes a young man, about six-foot-four with a snow- white smile. He can't be more than two, or three years older than me. "It's great you're here!" he says while we shake hands. "People from the mission have already told me about you." His openness and friendly welcome make our further conversation easy and natural. I didn't have to start off with an explanation of what I was doing here: he had been informed already from a letter, written by sister Christiane in Lyon, who had run the pediatrics department here for more than thirty years. The African doctor said her letter was a good enough recommendation. Soon we're talking business and the everyday running of the hospital.

"Oh, you are a surgeon? That's wonderful!" my colleague rejoices. "In the countryside, there are so few doctors that they can't afford to specialize. We find a way to deal with a wide variety of things here. The nearest surgeon is in the capital city. If you want to, you could take over the surgical ward," he adds. I am rather puzzled since I had expected to be working with an older, more experienced colleague. Nonetheless, I try to keep a stiff upper lip. When Lucien asks me to take a look at the surgical ward, I follow him.

The ward, which shares space with internal medicine, occupies the largest pavilion in the hospital. The rectangular building rises on a five-foot stone bedding, which secures the construction from oozing water, and keeps the ants from biting through. A veranda fringes the whole building and serves as a roofed hallway with entries to the individual rooms. The roof is made of corrugated iron. The walls are made of cement. The

The hospital itself consists of a complex of six low brick houses. (Page 39)

windows, which would normally have netting to keep mosquitoes from getting in, are basic wooden shutters without any glass panes.

There are only metal beds and small metal tables in the rooms. Nothing more. The relatives of the sick have to bring blankets, dishes, and petroleum lamps.

"I would like you to take a look at a patient I am going to operate on tomorrow." Lucien says, as we enter one of the rooms. The patient has some sort of a formation in her belly, and I want to find out what it is," he explains. The room is dark. There is a middle-aged woman lying on a poor bed. She seems to be studying me distrustfully. While performing a casual examination I do actually feel a smooth bump, about the size of a baby's head. "Could she possibly be pregnant?" I ask. "That's out of the question," my colleague laughs, "the last time she had a baby was ten years ago. Look, she is more than forty and that's the age of retirement in Africa." "And did you try the ultrasound?" I ask, remembering instantly a small sonogram unit I eyed in his study. "Well, I did," he admits. "You know, it doesn't resemble anything, but I'm still in training. We got the machine recently from one humanitarian organization." We agree to give it another try. The

41

outcome is startling. The screen shows the swollen uterus filled with something reminiscent of a snowstorm. "That can't be anything but mola," I ponder. Mola is a very rare disease, it occurs when the embryo turns into a tumor. I haven't cured this illness before, but I should be prepared for everything here in Africa. "Well then, how should we tackle it?" asks Lucien. "I don't know yet," I ruminate. I spend the evening searching through the medical books and textbooks I have brought with me, but there is no clear answer. A European doctor would cleanse the uterus, and monitor the woman's progress with regular checkups to help prevent a possible relapse. Here, however, I have no reason to believe that, once cured, the woman would ever return to the hospital for a checkup. Moreover, the checkups would be far beyond the potential of our small lab here. So, taking into account our restricted conditions and the age of the patient, the most viable solution is to remove the whole uterus with the tumor.

I suggest this to Lucien in the afternoon on the following day. He agrees. "Would you like to perform the operation with me?" he asks. "No, no," I refuse. "I would rather watch how you work here, but I would be willing to take care of the anesthesia during the procedure. "OK then, follow me. We'll start shortly." I follow him to a small house labeled "Bloc Opératoire".

There are two operating rooms, and a sterilization room in the building. I glance through the room. An inch wide slit gapes from under the door. There is a glassless window, with a mosquito net and white lamellas that could be tilted to avert the fierce sunshine. The wind keeps carrying red dust in from the outside. I hear the pigs grunting from underneath the window. "Where is your apparatus for anesthesia?" I say, searching in vain. "Nowhere." "And oxygen?" I say, turning a little perplexed. "Oh no, there's none," laughs Lucien. "You're not in Paris, you are in the bush!" "Well, I am looking forward to the operation then," I say to myself, doubtfully.

A middle-aged man of slight build and short hair enters the room. "Here comes Goum, the head nurse of the surgical ward."

Lucien introduces us. "He will be in charge of narcosis, and here comes my assistant Albert, the head nurse of the hospital." I heartily greet them both. They are both very respectful, but their mistrustful glances could hardly pass unnoticed. Now, looking back, I realize that this was one of the most important encounters of my African stay. Unlike the doctor, who was barely seen at the hospital because he was constantly away on business, the presence of the two men was indispensable. They have been striving to keep surgical ward going in the complicated African reality. Like other nurses, they received no salary in the past months due to the economic decline of the state. They maintained their places, however, because their conscience would not let them leave. And there was nobody to replace them.

My first impressions from the operation are ghastly. The patient wasn't linked up to a respiratory setup, because there wasn't any. The sedation was induced by injection of anesthetics into the vein. When the patient began to gain consciousness, she was given another dose and the process was repeated until the end of the operation. Now and again, Goum would measure her blood pressure with a simple cuff, and he kept track of her pulse by touch. The monitoring of the patient's respiration was ingeniously simple, too. She had a little fluff of cotton glued under her nose. As long as it moved, it showed that the patient was still breathing. In comparison to European standards, the operation was very bloody. The instruments and needles were huge; the sutures were thick. But the operation ran quite smoothly considering the conditions. "I don't think she will be recovering without complications." I say in disbelief once the operation is over. "Don't worry," Lucien comforts me. "The bush people are thick-skinned, they can bear a lot. By the way, there is another stumper I would like to show you before your departure tomorrow to Niem.

Again I follow him to one of the rooms. There is an aged woman lying on a bed. She is skinny and all wrapped up in rags. She seems to be in very bad condition. She's got a huge hernia exposing segments of intestine. There are two apertures in the abdomen through which intestinal liquid is seeping. "Good God, you can't possibly operate on this!" I look questioningly at Luciano. "There was a similar case in a hospital back home. The head consultant said he would perform an operation on the female patient only if her life were in danger, i.e. if intestinal obstructions occurred, so he sent her home. There was an intensive care unit with all the modern equipment where the convalescent patient would be taken care of. But this is out of the question. You've got nothing of that sort here," I try to talk Luciano out of the operation. "I know," he says, nodding his head gravely. The risks are immense, but the woman comes from a distant village, and she has already tried the local healers. She walked for more than 60 miles on foot to us here. She is reconciled that she will most probably die here. We are her last chance. She could never afford the private clinic in the capital. I am ready to do it. But you know more about surgery than I, it is your field, isn't it? So I think you should operate on her. "I guess he is right, but... After a pause I say, acquiesced "Well then, tomorrow. See you at the operating room in the afternoon." As I walk back to the mission, I recall Marcello's words of warning: "Remember, you haven't got a work permit, so stay out of everything. You could easily wind up in prison." Prison or no prison, we must try to save her. We must give it a try.

Chapter Seven

People from the Mission

It's already pitch dark as I stroll towards the mission. There is a group of people on the lighted veranda. Most of them are sisters from the neighborhood, who are waiting to greet me. I finally have a chance to meet all the remaining members of the mission.

Marie-René and Christiane are the oldest. They must both be over seventy. Marie-René used to work as a midwife. She was the first one to come to Bozoum more than forty years ago! She is one of the founders of the maternity ward. Christiane ran the pediatrics ward for more than thirty years. Both have left their previous professions, but continue to help out by serving the blind and elderly three times a week at the small mission infirmary. It is later that I learn that both Marie-René and Christiane were repeatedly given the opportunity to go back home to native France, and spend their last years in the peace and calm of the cloister. They both stayed, Africa grew to be their new home. In the French community, there are also sister Celine, who teaches sewing at the local school: two lessons a day, three times a week; and Ruphine, a Central-African, who cares for the kids of the local kindergarten. And then there are Mercedes and Marina, both from Uruguay, and Rosa from Italy. All three live in Bozoum, but they don't work here. They try to help the poor who live in nearby small villages in the bush. So, counting myself, we have people of six nationalities and of four continents. There is only a shortage of native Australians.

"When you get back from Niem, I am going to take you around and show you some patients," whispers Marina. "But I don't even know whether I am going to work here," I answer, insecurely. "See, I haven't received my work permit yet, and I might have to stay in Niem." "No, no. You must work here!" the nun resolutely shakes her head. "I will be praying for you." "We've been waiting for a doctor for years," adds Marcello, a little crankily. "And the only doctor here is constantly away on business, attending meetings and sittings, with almost no time left for patients!" I look at the people around me, and I can clearly picture today's entrance at the hospital. It's clear that if I stay in Bozoum, it won't work to sit and wait for a permit from a distant ministry. Neither the locals, nor my conscience will allow that.

46

Chapter Eight

Journey to Niem

Two days on the road. Father Sebastien drives me the first 100 miles to Bouar, and from there we continue with Angelo, the guy I had met on the plane in Paris before our departure to Africa. Angelo is a volunteer like me, and works here as a dentist. We still have a good sixty miles to drive. Niem is a small village in the mountains of the Yadé range near the border of Cameroon.

The surrounding landscape is monotonous, just bushes, low trees with sparse leaves, burnt grass and the ever-present red soil. Only the roads show a change; they keep getting worse. In order to manage 25 miles in one hour, you need a good car and a good driver. We are constantly dodging potholes and deep cracks. With a tight grip on the handholds, I try to keep from hitting the roof and the door. My eyelids are drooping; I am fighting to stay awake. I can't stop thinking about the operation, my Bozoum nightmare.

Again I recall the situation when I had to remove the sections of intestine grown to peritoneum, as well as a part of the intestinal wall with chronic fistulae. As the patient moved and began to moan, Goum would immediately inject a roughly measured dose of anesthetics into the vein. He would also attentively measure her blood pressure, and watch our "brilliant monitor" – the fluff of cotton glued underneath her nose. Thusly, he would make sure the patient was still breathing. During the operation I grew very fond of my African colleagues who, in the middle of the bush, have been struggling amidst conditions that were entirely unimaginable for a spoiled European surgeon. There are all kinds of difficulties; unbalanced anesthesia, no theatre nurse, huge needles, no myo-relaxation, a non-sufficiently aseptic environment, and the temperature in the operating room rising above 85F. Nevertheless, the operation was a success. After almost four hours I was able to take off my sweat-soaked shirt when I noticed Albert and Goum were smiling at me, and contentedly nodding their heads. Their looks had changed greatly in comparison to the day we had first met. I realized today's operation had been a sort of entrance exam.

Suddenly I soar from my seat, and hit the car roof. Then I open my eyes to see Angelo, all smiles. "Don't you have mufflers in the car?" "You're right, I don't," Angelo calmly replies, "they've been crying for repair for more than a few years." "And your car is real dirty, too!" I burst out, annoyed, trying to clean off my pants that used to be green, and now are orange-red. "I can't really close the back door," Angelo responds in amusement. "I am just a poor dentist, I am not a gold-bug like you in Bozoum."

"You know Tiziano, don't you?" I ask Angelo, in a friendly way again. "For a couple of years," nods the Italian. "He had originally studied medicine, and worked at the ward of internal medicine of some hospital in northern Italy, but then he made the decision to become a priest, and after ordination moved here to Africa." "Oh, he then works both as a doctor and a priest?" I inquire. "That's right. He serves mass in the morning, and then he locks

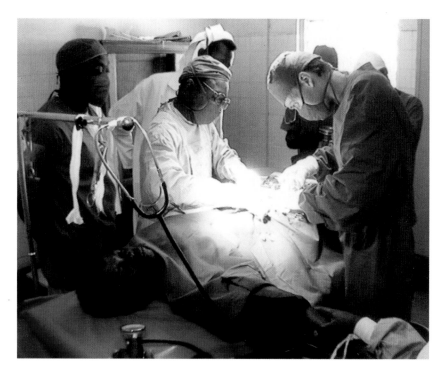

Unbalanced anesthesia, no theatre nurse, huge needles, no
myo-relaxation, a non sufficiently aseptic environment, and
the temperature in the operating room rising above 85F...

himself up in the hospital till the evening. He usually spends his
Saturdays and Sundays in the same fashion." Wait," I interrupt
Angelo, "Marcello told me there was only a dispensary, i.e. an
infirmary, and not a hospital in Niem." "Yes, you're right, agrees
the dentist, "it's always been merely an infirmary. The nearest
hospital is too far away from the village, so Tiziano added a few
rooms, giving the more difficult cases a place to stay over night.
Through all of this he is basically on his own. He's got an
assistant, who examines the blood and stool samples of the sick, a

midwife and two helpers who clean the facility and distribute medicine to the sick. The examining of patients, however, is solely his responsibility both night and day, as are the check ups of the hospitalized. Moreover, he must handle the supplies and repairs of his small hospital. By the way, I heard him saying in the transmitter that he was looking forward to meeting you. I guess you understand why." I see what's on Angelo's mind, but I am afraid I won't be of much help to Tiziano. I don't know the local customs and problems, or their methods of treatment. I don't know the language either.

"I would be very happy if he taught me some Sango," I say after some silence. "Tiziano is the right person," Angelo confirms my decision, nodding. "Tiziano is regarded here as a linguist of some distinction. His command of Sango is brilliant, but he also speaks Fufulbe, the immensely difficult language of the nomadic M'Bororo: there are lots of them here up north. "But Sango should suffice, it's the official language here together with French and all Central Africans should comprehend," I argue. "But who told you that the M'Bororo are of Central Africa?" The Italian dentist bursts into laughter. "Most of them have no stable abode, they are nomads, and just like in the past centuries, they drive their animals through the bush, carrying all they need on the animals' backs. They have no notion of a state border. During the dry season they drive their animals southwards, to the Central African rainforests, and in the rain season they return north to Chad or Cameroon. Their language is similar Swahili on the eastern coast of Africa. It's spoken in a great part of sub-Saharan Africa, from Niger to Sudan. Unlike Sango, of which there is no written record until the arrival of the French, Fufulbe has actually two forms – it employs both the Roman, and Arabic alphabet. It's a very intricate language. For example, they use two entirely different words for a thing in singular and in plural. I would love to learn the language, too" Angelo expatiates, with enthusiasm. "Well, I guess Sango will do just fine for me," I interrupt him. "Yes, you have to start off with Sango," the Italian agrees, making no objections, then remarks: "Tiziano's got his proven methods, you'll see. He did succeed in teaching a few of us."

While the two of us are talking, the landscape markedly changes. There are less bushes and trees and more tall, dry grass. Sometimes, as our view widens, we can see the bushy hills dragging far off into the horizon. The road we follow keeps going up on a long, mountain ridge. We have already reached the hills of the Yadé mountain range, which borders with Cameroon on the northwest of the country. As we are approaching Niem, the sun begins to set, and the air cools very slowly after the hot day.

Chapter Nine

A Village in the Mountains

We arrive in Niem late in the afternoon. It is a small, secluded village, located almost at the top of the ridge of the Yadé mountain range about 4000 feet above sea level, near the Cameron border. The elevation doesn't really mark the appearance of the landscape. The inhabitants, however, must surely feel this during the dry season, as the temperature differences between night and day grow considerably. The sun at noon is such a furnace, one can hardly walk out. The quicksilver on the thermometer shows 95F. At night the temperature lowers to 60F. And if Hartaman – the night wind – blows, as it usually does, the morning temperatures may be even lower. This is "icy cold" for both the locals, and the whites that have already spent some time in Africa. Early in the morning, one can see ragged families huddling together around campfires. The more moneyed ones usually wear ski caps and old, long coats.

Angelo pulls up at the yard of the tiny mission that stands at the middle of the village. The mission consists of a single small house. Although the yard is fenced, the gate is always open wide, so the villagers, especially the youngest ones, feel free to wander without restraint between the village and the mission.

Our arrival doesn't escape their attention of course. Soon we are surrounded by a clump of kids who attentively examine both us, and our car. Angelo is really busy in shielding his beloved "little Toyota". Father Tiziano has just walked into the yard with a smile. He is about fifty, of a smaller build, with grayish hair and thick glasses. At first glance, he doesn't look like a priest at all. He's wearing a fair shirt and an old worn out pair of jeans. "Glad you're here," he welcomes us cordially, "I've got work for you! Starting from tomorrow," he adds, as he perceives how dirty and weary we are.

I get a room of my own. It's spacious and modestly furnished. On the concrete floor there is a wooden table, a chair, a wardrobe, and a bed with a mosquito net. There is a similar net on the window, and a simple shower in the corner. I am happy that after fourteen days of wandering from one place to another, I can finally unload my luggage and settle in somehow in Africa. The first thing I do is to check the whole room as a precautionary measure. It turns out to be the right thing. I find a couple of huge hairy spiders underneath my bed, and – although I am an amateur – I consider them poisonous; Angelo helps me dispose of them immediately.

The next day, Tiziano and I set out for the local hospital. The low one-floor building built of concrete and roofed with corrugated iron is about 1/8 mile from the mission. In the left section, there is a large room with eight beds and a birth hall. On the right, there is Angelo's office and consulting room, a lab, dentist's ward and a storeroom. A couple of small houses with hay roofs rise behind the building, they are built mainly of the cheap traditional clay bricks. These houses serve as an extension to the hospital. The number of patients keeps growing and there is desperately little money for more permanent buildings and for their maintenance.

On the compacted earth surrounding these houses, there camp relatives of the sick, who prepare food on small fireplaces. I can see many shepherds of the M'Bororo tribe. They are not hard to distinguish from the Central Africans. They are all of a very slender build, they have long arms and legs and oblong faces. Their skin is black, but their facial features are quite different from the Central Africans. Their Arabic features make them relatives of the ethnics up north. Their clothing, too, is louder. Men, as true Moslems, cover their heads with fez and often wear the long Arabic burnus. Their women, unlike the women in Arabic countries, don't cover their face. They are well known for their elegance. Beads interweave their diligently arranged hair, and they wear numerous bracelets, huge shiny earrings and colorful clothes. Most of them have made-up eyes, and some even wear special tattoos on their foreheads and cheeks.

"Sanu – Greetings!" Tiziano approaches them in a friendly manner as we pass by. The men turn, lift both arms up to head level, and with their palms facing us they give a slight bow. "Sanu," they reply jointly. Tiziano turns to me, and whispers: "The local Central Africans usually regard the M'Bororo as an inferior race, but in reality they are wonderful people." I could verify the truth of his words many times later on. They are true Moslems, but they lack the fanaticism existing in the Near East. Most of them never went to school, they don't speak French, and only a little Sango, but they have maintained a great sense for duty and fair play. When a M'Bororo promised something, I could be sure he would keep his word. The people are exceptionally resilient, used to the tough conditions of nomadic life. I had the privilege to operate on them a few times. They were stone-faced when putting up with pain, and would never complain. They reminded me somewhat of the romanticized image of the North American Indians. Unfortunately, their lifestyle is undergoing severe changes under the pressure of modern civilization. Their family bonds are slowly breaking up as the young M'Bororo discover the advantages of life without migration, and sell the inherited herds... So vanishes the old Africa. It is a pity.

Tiziano unlocks the infirmary. Mothers with small babies on their back, wrapped in bandanas, are the first to rush in. Baby carriages are unknown here.

M'Bororo women, unlike the women in
Arabic countries, don't cover their face.
They are well known for their elegance.

"Marcel, you take care of three patients and examine them and find out what's the matter. I will take another three. If you need help or something, tell me," Tiziano organizes our work. But before we launch into our work, he calls his helper: "Elie, come here to translate for Marcel."

Tiziano seldom sends his patients to the lab, his diagnoses rely only
on the patient's explication and the classic clinical examination, i.e.
looking, knocking, hearing and touching.

There are many sick. There is neither enough time nor
resources to grant a laboratory examination to all of them.
Tiziano seldom sends his patients to the lab, his diagnoses rely
solely on the patient's explication and the classic clinical
examination, i.e. looking, knocking, hearing and touching. It is
the old medical art, which in Europe has been slowly
disappearing. Doctors today make less and less use of their senses,
they are equipped by a variety of more precise instruments and
methods. There is a lack of these here, however.

I observe Tiziano for a moment and then I begin examining
my own patients. I feel insecure. It's much worse than I had
expected. The first woman has been telling me about her
troubles for about two minutes but I can't understand a word.
"What did she say?" I turn to my interpreter. "She's got a stomach

ache," Elie impassively sums up her long speech. I am desperate. How can I reach a diagnosis with this information? It is the details that I need to know – how long have the pains lasted, where and how intensive they are, what causes the pain and what relieves it, etc. There's no other way but to ask again. Elie translates my questions and then the patient's replies. It is evident he does not share my obsession with details, and tends to give me just brief summaries of her problems. Soon he grows tired of this, too. "What's this bloody" mundjou- white's "problem? He doesn't speak a word of Sango…" I can read this in his eyes.

I don't know much about the cure of local diseases yet, but I am not a total beginner – I have four years of experience in Czech hospitals and a three-month course in tropical medicine in Lyon. The reality of work in this non-European environment, however, clashes with my previous existing know-how I received from various medical textbooks. Another proof of this is my next patient.

The child has had a fever for two days, but there are no other signs that would indicate a concrete illness like pneumonia, middle ear inflammation or meningitis. In Europe, this would be labeled as a common virus disease to be cured by anti-fever tablets, vitamins and plenty of water. "What do you think about it?" I ask Tiziano, "Will Paracetamol and water do?" "You should include the Malaria treatment – the Nivaquin tablets," the Italian advises me readily. "So you think it is Malaria?" I ask him again. "Well, I don't know," Tiziano shrugs his shoulders, "but I know that with every fever here you must take malaria into account, unless you can totally rule it out. Ruling it out would require repeated blood examinations – and considering the number of patients and our resources here – that is entirely unattainable. If there is a chance that the child has malaria and you don't administer a proper cure, you may have jeopardized his life.

In the evening I return to the mission, absolutely jaded. This was a hard day. Not only did we examine a few dozen patients, but we had to do the rounds in the ward as well. There were a vast number of cases I had not encountered in Europe before. I saw a woman with AIDS, who suffered from herpes that did not only affect a section of skin – like in most cases – but her whole body; a man with tuberculosis that seized both the lungs, and the stomach; another man with mold that thoroughly overgrew his legs. In this forgotten part of the world, there was so much poverty and so much suffering around!

I feel terribly weary, and also like an idiot. Today has dented my self-confidence. There is a lot to learn, if I want to be of any help to Tiziano. I must start off with the language.

"Tiziano, I hear you used to teach Sango!" I say before dinner. "I taught some sisters," he admits, "but you need it too, don't you?" he gives me a smile as he sees my weary and worried look. "So join me in the kitchen after dinner and bring your Bible with you." I don't understand. Why a Bible? I come to the given place at the given time, bringing – as this was Tiziano's wish – a tiny, pocket edition Bible, printed in Czech. Tiziano is expecting me already. At the table before him, there is a book. It also is a Bible, but it is printed in Sango. Now everything clears up: the comparative method, of course. There is no other option. There are no real textbooks of Sango in French, let alone in Czech. You might come across some Sango-French dictionaries, usually printed in the colonization period, and some small notebooks with common phrases in Sango published by the missionaries themselves. That's about it.

Tiziano opens his Bible to the beginning of the Book of Luke. We start reading the first sentences. Thanks to the Czech translation I understand the meaning perfectly. Day after day we analyze clause after clause, discuss the sentence structure, and the meaning of single words. Tiziano translates common questions and directions of a doctor for me as well. Slowly I grow into the logic of the language and soon I am able to glue words into simple sentences. I realize the grammar of the vernacular isn't too difficult. The nouns have no declension, the verbs don't conjugate, and words are simply lined up one after another. If you want to say "You will go to the market tomorrow", you say "Kekerekeh moh gah nah galah" meaning in Sango "Tomorrow you go market". The words that have more meanings are tricky. When they use, e.g. the expression "bi" in the noun position it means "night", but once placed in the verb position, it means "to throw". There are also plenty of short, ambiguous words in Sango, and the listener won't figure out the meaning of the sentence, unless he pays close attention to the word order. Words that could be pronounced in different ways also make things more intricate. For example, "walah – to work" could be pronounced, and written also as "warah", without a shift in meaning, however.

I dare to place Sango among the easier languages. But still, learning the language – at least the beginnings – is a drag.

I regard the following days in Niem as the most difficult of my entire African stay. Every day I struggled with the strange language, and cured illnesses I had never encountered before. I was growing used to the extreme heat of the day, and the cold of the night; I was getting accustomed to life in mission, and a new diet. Although I wasn't left with the food of the natives, the plain and modest Italian menu was rather distant from Czech cuisine. Father Tiziano was busy from dawn to dusk, and found little time for cooking. A woman from the village would regularly come to the mission and prepare something to eat. She was no professional cook, the food was virtually the same every day – vegetable soup and boiled pasta. The pasta for Italian missionaries was imported from Europe twice a year. I guess no Italian could ever do without it.

We would occasionally eat some chicken, which was easy to buy in the village. But please don't picture a scented, crispy, golden juicy chicken with stuffing like we eat at home. Here we had to cope with a boiled one that was so slim that we were practically left with only the bones to lick. On occasion we would try something different, like beef, antelope or snake. Tropical fruit would rule the table. It grew all around and cost almost nothing at the market. But bread! That was a rarity. Every three weeks, Angelo, the dentist, would bring a few loaves from Bouar. We were eating them gradually, not really minding the fact that they grew stale and all maggoty by ants. Every morning by breakfast I would first break the bread into small bits, pick out the ants and dip it in tea so it would soften. Apart from tea and milk we drank filtered water. I used to pour it from a huge tank in the kitchen into my own plastic bottle several times a day. The heat of the tropics causes the body to lose a great amount of liquid; it's thus necessary to drink a lot – at least a gallon a day, even if you don't feel thirsty. Once you fail to follow this regime, you notice it on your performance. You soon feel tired and weakened. Then a migraine joins in, and then fever, and finally you can get cramps in your muscles, or end up with kidney complications, though you mightn't have suffered from kidney stones before.

What caused me more trouble than heat and temperature fluctuation was the terrible dryness here. Every evening I would go under my mosquito net with a bottle of filtered water; the thirst would wake me up a couple of times during the night. In total darkness I would be clumsily reaching for my flashlight to find the bottle.

Falling asleep wasn't easy. Hartaman, the desert wind, was blowing all night through the shutters, bringing heaps of dust, dryness and death. It's hard to tell the reason why, but each year in the dry season, there is an immense increase of meningitis in the whole sub-Saharan belt. Its victims are mostly children. After my arrival, the epidemic was just beginning and there have been only a few cases as yet.

After a week of working together, Tiziano gradually let me work alone. He used his free time to eventually sort out the medicaments and medical supplies. Being at the infirmary by myself really wasn't easy; I was left only with my African assistants. They were polite, but at the same time evidently incredulous. And, moreover, they were unhappy everything took so long. Talking through the interpreter was ponderous and I was rather inexperienced in fixing the diagnosis by only "having a squint at the patient as he enters the room."

In a few days, father Tiziano left for Bouar for four days and all the responsibility for the infirmary fell on my shoulders. This was not enviable. As I went to check the ward block, the midwife took me straight to a woman who gave birth to a dead child in the night. "She was bleeding a bit, doctor," she said and pointed to a bucket half-filled with clotted blood. I looked at the woman who had just given birth. She had pale palms and cold sweat was standing out on her forehead, and I could hardly feel her pulse. "She must get blood, immediately." I said with certain firmness, "so before you take time to draw any from her relatives, give her an infusion." Shortly, the midwife ran up to me helplessly and said: "It doesn't work, I can't find her vein, I did all I could." I took the needle and tried it myself. Unfortunately, the patient had lost so much blood that her veins had completely collapsed. Her state was worsening. She was rapidly lapsing into shock. "And now? If we fail to find the vein, she will die!" the midwife lamented. "I shall then excise the vein. Please bring me the sterile instruments" I stopped her moan. Dead silence followed. The midwife's eyes popped in surprise: "There is nothing of that sort here, no operations have ever been here." "But, I guess you do sew up a cut now and then, don't you?" "Well, now and then, yes," the woman admitted. "Yes, there must be some scissors, a scalpel, and a pair of tweezers. But you say sterile? No way." "So bring it all, and also a metal tray and alcohol." The woman stared in wonder. Then she nodded, and ran away. She was right back. Bringing with her both the things, and other helpers. "What's about to happen here?" I read in their curious looks.

The only possibility to obtain sterile instruments in the bush is to heat them up to high temperature. I poured some alcohol into the bottom of the tray, placed the metal instruments on it and set the alcohol on fire. There appeared a little, bluish flame above the tray. Then I grabbed the tray on sides, and rocked it. A flame flared up, much bigger than before. It had an orange glow. To put it bluntly, I flambéed the instruments in front of their eyes, just like meat is flambéed before the guests in a luxurious restaurant. It was a real sensation. They were all pushing around me. After the impressive start, I put on my gloves, deadened the place at the inner ankle, and excised the vein, inserted a cannula, which I then connected to the infusion. My colleagues' initial astonishment burst out to great joy. They have never seen something like that before. All of a sudden, I transformed from a "mundju" – a white man, who doesn't understand the language, to a "doctor of renown".After repeated transfusions, the patient recovered and she walked out of the hospital in a couple of days. After the incident, the local personnel started to take me seriously, and we would readily collaborate.

Not all the patients recovered. I can still remember as parents brought in a young Arabian boy with a severe form of malaria. They laid him on the table, but before I could give him medicine, he died in front of my eyes. I can also remember a one-year-old boy with a brain infection; I would give him injections for several nights. I had to do this by myself – Tiziano's assistants administered the drugs only in the morning and in the evening and went back home to their families for the night.

Night after night the mission watchman would wake me up, and accompany me to the hospital. I was really tired after my all-day work, my eyelids were falling, but I recall the night sky with thousands of stars shining at the hay-roofs of the Niem village. I would follow the night watchman, who groped around with a kerosene lamp in one hand, and a snake-stick in the other. He wore a woolen hat over his ears, and wrapped himself up in a long, old coat as protection against the strong, cold wind. We would sneak into the room, where both the patients and their relatives slept, having shelter from the cold of the night. Under the weak kerosene light, I would dilute the medicine, and inject it into the kid's little bottom. Although the lamp illuminated only part of the room, I saw the shiny, observant and silent eyes of the natives. However, I never heard the slightest remark or complaint about them being disturbed from their rest. Unfortunately, and despite all my effort, the little boy fell into a coma in a few days, and died shortly after. I considered this my personal failure, and I had to cope with it for some time.

But I don't want to write only about sad stories: there are a lot of joyful ones! I did manage to cure many patients whose illnesses were often very severe. I happily cast my mind back on a few-week-old baby: a healer had poured a boiling nostrum in his ear, and burnt half of his face. It all turned out well though – the child healed up in our hospital.

Once some parents brought in a young girl, who had stuck a stone in her ear a few days before. It had sunk far, and then the inflammation had set in, causing quite a bit of pain to the girl. She wouldn't even let me touch her ear. In order to remove the stone, I first had to put her to sleep with anesthetic. I did not realize then, what a stir this would create among the Africans. They had never seen a patient under narcosis yet, nor had they even heard of it, too. Father Tiziano isn't a surgeon and he never employs total narcosis.

While my assistants were carrying the lifeless girl outside so she would wake up from narcotic sleep among her family, an upheaval arose. In a moment, all of her family pushed inside the office, all willing to avenge the "dead baby". It cost my collaborators a lot of effort and sweat to calm down the petrified, rattled and shocked relatives and ensure them everything was ok, that the child was fine, and that she would awaken from narcosis shortly.

My best memories are of the small, big-eyed and curious, little black children of the village. I was for them something totally new and unknown. It wasn't hard to make friends with them. As I was coming back to the mission house the first evening, about twenty of them were playing at my door. They were waiting for my arrival from the hospital, to observe me, to find out what I was like. I got the idea to dig a yoyo out of my suitcase. I sat myself on my doorstep, and I began to play with it, stealthily watching their reactions. Soon they were all standing around me. They were watching the yoyo returning back to my hand, and they were pointing at it with their fingers, laughing. I stopped, and asked the nearest boy: "Moh tarah. – Try it." He grasped the toy carefully in his fingers, and tried to spin down it and then catch it again. It didn't work out. All the others were rolling about in laughter, and wanted to try it also. I let them play. The smallest girl then ventured to approach me, and using her little finger, started to examine whether the white color really sticks to my skin. No wonder. The swarthy Italians were the only whites she could have met at the mission, and they were all well tanned due to their long stay below the African sun. A man with blond hair and blue eyes definitely must have seemed funny to her. I smiled at her and handed her a candy. I gave candy to all the others, and then I left for my own business.

I discovered them at my door again the next day. They were all barefoot; the smallest dressed only in tiny shirts. Laughing, they demanded a "yeh tih ngia", which could be translated as "a funny thing". I new straight away they were asking for the yoyo. Every evening since, they would come to play at my door again. They would always scratch at my door and whimper: "Much nah obi bonbon. – Give me candy."

One day I spotted the boys sitting under the mango tree by the road. Armed with slings, they were watching the treetop with attention. Wham – a stone flew among the branches. Something fell down from the tree. I went closet to see the kill. It was a huge locust. The little hunters immediately tore off its legs and wings, and ate it right then and there. The triumphant shooter smiled happily and proudly.

One day they even tried to hunt me. Hidden in tall grass, they were shooting small reed arrows at me. They were not too successful: the wind was strong and the arrows were light. I called for them, grasped two reed sticks, bound them together at a right angle and stretched a plastic bag over it. A tail made of paper, and the dragon was ready! I showed them how to fly it. They understood at once, crazy about the new entertainment. But the dragon flew badly. Strong wind broke the sticks after a while. "There is nothing I can do about it," I shrugged my shoulders. At first, the little boys merely eyed me with their huge, disappointed, eyes, but then they vehemently claimed all the remnants of the dragon, the strings and the plastic. After dinner, I walked to the

I discovered them at my door again
the next day.

yard, I looked up, and high above the clouds I saw a dragon flying. The bright kids had substituted feeble reed with pliable wood, and so they constructed a new dragon, a much better one than its predecessor. And most importantly: It flew.

About three weeks have passed since my arrival. Tiziano has just returned from a several-day trip to the capital; he had left to

One day they even tried to hunt me.

pick up a group of friends who had come to visit him. He had breaking news for me: "Marcel, apart from buying medicine I went to the health ministry to see how they were managing with your work permit. Can you imagine they haven't started dealing with your request yet?" I was dumbfounded. "What? But I had sent my request, copies of my diploma, and other certificates with translations a half a year before my departure to Africa! Tiziano smiled indulgently. "This is the way it works here: if you want something from the authorities, you must stay at the spot and keep urging them repeatedly. You should set out for Bangui, as soon as you can."

Thus ended my stay in Niem. I was ready to leave any time. So after long good-byes with the members of the mission and the local citizens, my little friends inclusive, Angelo drove me to Bouar the very next day. I was lucky. Enrico, the carpenter, was just getting ready to set out for Bozoum. I was happy to catch him still. I felt uneasily during the journey, mainly because I caught a viral infection from my patients. I didn't stay in Bozoum for long. Just for the night and the next day I proceeded to the capital with Marcello – for a change. We got there late in the afternoon. I drove about 500 miles through the bush within the two days. Today, at the beginning of February, I face the same situation as one month ago. I am in Bangui again, without my passport, my visa and my work permit: just like back then.

Chapter Ten

Back in the Capital City

It's the middle of February. The mercury on the thermometer has climbed to 100 F. There hasn't been a drop of rain in the past three months. The city is a scorcher; the hot air is shimmering above the dusty streets. The nearby rainforests breath out their humidness, and the atmosphere of the city is getting almost unbearable. I lie under my mosquito net in the Centre d'accueil and I cannot fall asleep. I've been awaiting the coldness of the night, in vain. It's 10 pm, midnight, 2 am… still the same heat and the same sultriness. I feel drops of sweat rolling down my cheeks. My pillow is all wet. About 4 am, it's finally getting a little cooler. The Sun rises at 6, however, and the mercury starts climbing up again. All the citizens of Bangui are torpid, irritated, and tired out by the heat. They're all eagerly waiting for the first rain. I wish I were in Bozoum now. The air there is much dryer, cooler and nicer than in Bangui during this season.

The only thought running through my head at night is: let's settle this as quickly as we can, and then we can get away, away from this burning hell. It seems Marcello, too, is of a similar opinion.

Early in the morning we undertake the first steps. First of all, we find out at the health ministry about my visa. It takes us enough time to fight our way through the small clerks to the office of the deputy minister. I had been naively expecting that after I give them the reason of my visit and hand in the required documents, my working visa was finally going to be settled, but I was wrong. The clerk smiled at me politely, but it wasn't hard to guess he didn't feel like listening to me, and he wouldn't deal with my problem at all. He merely advised me to join the local General Medical Council, and wait to see what would happen next. The office of the Medical Council wasn't hard to find. It stood right next to the Ministry. It was a small, dilapidated building, full of unpleasant clerks. They heard me out and read through my papers, including my Charles University diploma written in Latin, after which they dismissed me sternly: "You need to obtain an official translation of the language." "But it's Latin – the classical language of doctors all around the world," I object. "Well, we weren't aware of that here," the man shrugged it off, handing all my papers back to me. But where can I find an official translator of Latin, here in Africa? Well, I am not going to start writing to Prague, waiting weeks and weeks for an answer! I feel really disappointed and morose. I have been running around with the local authorities all morning, having arguments with disagreeable clerks. But I brought all the papers required for the work permit with me, and their French translation from Czech, too. There is not a whit of goodwill from the side of the authorities. This is what I don't understand. I came to Africa to help people in regions where there are no doctors, and I claim

"This is the oldest mission in the country, founded in 1894," Marcello starts off with a historical exposition.

no pay for this. Then I recall the warm welcome of the African doctor and nurses in Bozoum. Is it so, that the clerks in the capital don't give a damn about the countryside? It was later that I finally understood. All the state clerks have received no salary for the past few months. Their doings – with nothing to stimulate them – are then, of course, at minimum level. Marcello gave me a victorious wink: "We are going to manage. I speak decent Latin, it's no problem for me to translate it, and the archbishop will give us the stamp. He speaks Latin, too, and what's more, he is African, so nobody questions his authority here." That's a weight off my mind, I confess. We set out for the archbishopric. It's not far. On a small mound reaching above the river Oubangui, there is a group of low buildings of fired brick with tin roofs. All houses are built in colonial style, peeping from a jungle of tropical plants and trees. "This is the oldest mission in the country, founded in 1894," Marcello starts off with a historical exposition. "This was only five years after the first whites, French soldiers, got here

70

upstream of the Congo River, and found the first military station at the rapids. They named it simply "Bangui" which denotes "rapids" in the Sango vernacular. Throughout the century, this small station has grown into a capital city of half a million inhabitants. The Central African Republic is thus known in Europe only for a short period, especially the regions out of Bangui. Until the end of WWII, the French had been building up a network of military and commercial stations in the country, which had been originally called Oubangui-Chari. Not until the inter-war period, however, did France gain real control over the colony. Still in 1925 in Boccaranga – a small town in the vicinity of Bozoum – the prominent market would take place, where rich Arabians from the Sahel region bought black slaves from Arabian slave-hunters. Then the French finally succeeded in suppressing the slave trade." Thinking my grandmother was a pupil then, it doesn't really seem too long ago.

Slowly we drive up the lengthy hillock. "What are these crosses?" I ask, pointing at a small cemetery on the left. "The first missionaries are buried there, they started coming here at the turn of the century. They were usually young, and they were dying young, too. In most cases, malaria was the cause. "Once more I turn my head to see the small, sprouted cemetery, and we arrive in the grounds of the mission. Marcello pulls up his Mitsubishi in the middle of the yard, facing a very plain, small church, with a low tower, not plastered, and built of fired brick. "That's the church of Saint Paul's," he remarks, "the oldest sacral building in the country, more than a hundred years old."

We get out of the car and walk slowly toward the tower; a beautiful view of the river opens before us. The hills on the other bank of Oubangui are already part of the Congo. The hills are all green with trees and bushes reaching to the very banks of the river. Pirogues are drifting along, golden shafts of setting sun reflect on the water, and there are hammering rapids in the distance, that bestowed their name to the City. Compared to the dusty streets underneath, smothered by unbearable noise, inconceivably chaotic traffic, and heaps of trash, this clean, calm and flowery place that creates an atmosphere of colonial Africa, seems like a true oasis. I fell in love at first sight with this beautiful part of Bangui.

I didn't even notice that Marcello disappeared for a while. "We can enter now," he said as he walked out of the archbishopric. I think I will always remember the warm welcome we received there. The archbishop attentively listened to us and then he readily confirmed the correctness of our translation. When he learned I was Czech, he immediately recalled the name of our president Václav Havel. Then he began to talk about the occupation of my country in 1968, and he even mentioned the Vltava River running through Prague. I must say I was surprised and much pleased – in the middle of Africa – by his familiarity with my country. I didn't think I would meet another person of the same sophistication as the archbishop during my stay here. "May I offer you a drink?" And before we manage to answer, cool lemonade is brought to us.

From a window, I study the green hills of Africa on the opposite bank. "Congo is so very near, and there is a war, isn't there?" I ask the archbishop, who sullenly nods and then quietly says: "The opposite bank is occupied by the rebels fighting against the general Kabila in Kinshasa. The rebels are not void of good will, however. They struggle to develop functioning infrastructure in the conquered regions, and they fight against the suppression of human rights. Once and again, Kabila has them bombarded with his planes, and one can hear the blasting bombs even from here. The war has been dragging on for several years, and its end is beyond sight. The rebels are of the same ethnic group as the Central Africans, who secretly support them. Who knows what effects this is about to have in our country..."

How truthful were his words! About four months later, Kabilo's army took possession of tankers transporting oil up the

We had to heat up our instrument sterilizer on a wooden stack.

Congo and Oubangui River, from the Bay of Guinea to the Central African Republic. The main supply route was thus cut off, and, all of a sudden, the country was facing a severe oil crisis. There was simply no oil. It could be purchased only on the black market for enormous costs. The only possibility left was to import oil by trucks on clay roads – and for hundreds of miles – from Cameroon. Hard times struck the country. We would feel the lack of oil even in Bozoum. As there was no more gas to feed the generator, the whole town was left without electricity. Even in the hospital we used kerosene lamps at night, our ultrasound would not work, and we had to heat up our instrument sterilizer on a wooden stack. This would still be all right, until the pump of the town's waterworks ran out of gas as well. The hospital was then left without water. It had to be drawn on and carried from wells, and it had to be boiled... The summer I spent in the Bozoum hospital was just about the worst period of my entire African stay.

At this moment, however, neither we, nor the archbishop sense what awaits us in near future. We discuss the political situation for a little while, and then we say goodbye, and we head back in good spirits to the Centre d'accueil. We are glad we managed at least a little progress with the whole affair.

As we are approaching the mission, the whole sky is frighteningly overcast. An unusual dimness surrounds us. The wind rises and clouds of dust scurry down the streets. When we enter the yard, Marcello sighs with relief: "We've made it on time," and then, talking from experience, he says: "It's about to rain." I stay underneath the veranda in front of the kitchen, watching the raging elements. The wind keeps rising, and it bends the mighty treetops more and more. Black clouds race down the sky. Wham! The first bolt of lightening has parted the sky. There is no rain yet. A tropical storm is near. Finally, the first heavy drops of rain hit the tin roof of the veranda. Then all at once, cords of rain pour from the sky, dribbling in small strands from the grooves of the corrugated iron roof, creating thus a perfect and coherent water grating before me. The whole yard suddenly turns into a huge puddle. Then a cook in an apron rushes out of the open kitchen door. His face is full of ecstatic joy. He raises his arms, exposes his face to the rain, and then he starts dancing in the puddles from joy. I lean back on the kitchen door, and delightfully inhale the fresh air. I watch the cook, and inwardly, I feel joy with him. I have been in Bangui only for two days so far, but I can understand his feelings well.

The next day I hand over the confirmed translation of my diploma – with all the other documentation – at the Medical Council. I leave the place with a promise, that my request shall be discussed at the next meeting. We can finally leave the capital, and return back to the Bozoum mission.

However, as it turned out later, the "discussing" did not take place for quite a while. A couple of months passed before I received the official request. Fortunately, after my Bozoum arrival, my colleague from the local hospital, doctor Baté, took responsibility, and – being the chairman of the health service in the prefecture of Ouham-Pendé – he issued a written permit that allowed me to practice medicine at his hospital. Although this didn't really go by the book, I could finally start working legitimately in Africa.

Chapter Eleven

One Day in Bozoum

With no telephone, television or Internet at hand, the Bozoum days are passing by slowly and calmly. Some of them are sad, some are happier, but most of them are very much alike.

6am

The sound of the church bell awakens me. The night watchman announces to everyone in Bozoum that a new day has begun.

I stay in bed a few more minutes, and then I roll out of my mosquito net, quickly put on my clothes and rush to the veranda, which offers a superb view of all of Bozoum. The early morning is really pleasant – it's only about 70F. The Sun is rising fast above the Binot Hill, and it melts away the morning mist. In the valley below the mission, hundreds of hay roofs mingle with the tops of the dark green mango trees, their boughs now bending under

"There is nothing to do about it, now you are the boss. The hospital is yours." Then Lucien left. (Page 78)

the load of ripe fruit. It's the first days of April, "the mango season". Looking at all the ripe fruit, I realize how time here really flies. I've been here for three months already. When I first arrived in Bozoum, the mango trees were in bloom.

7am

Breakfast is plain: powdered milk, marmalade, and local bread, which tastes a little funny: the bakers of Bozoum often add sugar instead of salt. Considering my Niem days, I feel like I am in an expensive restaurant.

I can't spend much time at breakfast. I am in a rush, as I am at the hospital by myself again. This isn't out of the ordinary, however. A week after I got back from my trip – running errands in Bangui – at the beginning of February, my African colleague doctor Baté came to see me, telling me he had been called for an important meeting at the capital city. After that he was going to set out for another meeting in Bossangoa. He merely shrugged his shoulders, gave me a smile and said apologetically: "There is nothing to do about it, now you are the boss. The hospital is yours." Then he left.

And this would happen again and again so – no wonder – that in the past two months we worked together for about a fortnight. The constant duties of administration leave him with virtually no time for his patients. To manage both of the two is truly beyond one's strength!

I finish my breakfast quickly. It doesn't rain today. The rain gave me an hour extra – neither the patients, nor the nurses hurry to the hospital in the rain. They sit tight, hoping for it to stop.

7.40am

Shortly after 7.40 I get into my small Citroën CV3, and leave for the hospital. I drive slowly – the road is jammed with potholes and stones. A small Czech flag on the rear mirror is swinging to and fro – Marina, a nurse, has sewn it recently for me.

I pass by the villagers heading to the market. They turn towards the car and greet me warmly. They are mostly women, carrying manioc, vegetables, peanuts, bananas, and plenty of other fruits in huge vessels on their heads. Most of them also carry babies, wrapped in bandanas on their backs. Kids, rushing to school, wave, smile, and holler at me: "Barah, mon docteur – Hello, Doctor."

7.50am

It's not a long drive. Before eight, I steer into the hospital yard, and pull up in the shade facing the operation hall. As I am getting out of the car, I can see – underneath the mighty mango trees, in the middle of the yard – the relatives preparing breakfast

Relatives prepare breakfast for their sick on small fireplaces.

for their sick on small fireplaces, while the others are still lying on mats, or having a chat. The site slowly begins to flurry with activity. Quickly I put on my white cloak, and hurry to the wards.

I start at the surgical ward. First of all – it is a local custom – I say hello to everyone, we shake hands, then I set out on my rounds. The head of the ward – major Goum, accompanies me. He is an immensely pleasant and competent man, and I can rely on him for everything.

In the past three months, we have become real friends. Not only does he take excellent care of the surgical ward, but he also handles the anesthesia for the patients I operate on. He works night and day. It happened many times that I needed to operate instantly, at night, and I went to his hut to wake him up. He would never complain. He would just get up, take his flashlight and rush off to the hospital with me. Only once did he mutter so much as a comment about it: "I have three children, doctor, and I want eight. But I think that as long as you are here, I won't have more than the three. "

I am satisfied with the round. Everything is all right at the ward. Even the young Arab, who got stabbed in the stomach in a city brawl three days ago, is now feeling better. I had to improvise when dealing with the lung injury. I took my stethoscope, and listened to the patient's respiration. The lung had opened already, and there was no sign of blood in the thorax. It seems my primitive drainage device – made of a urine catheter, a finger

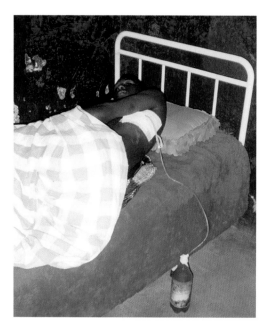

It seems my primitive drainage device – made of a urine catheter, a finger from a rubber glove, and an empty lemonade bottle – has been working perfectly.

from a rubber glove, and an empty lemonade bottle – has been working perfectly.

Despite bad hygiene and the hospital being insufficiently equipped, there is a very small post-operation death rate. I would not ascribe this as much to my abilities: it is the rather unbelievable resilience of the patients and a virtual absence of the normal illnesses associated with civilization, such as ischemic heart disease, or diabetes.

I allowed two cured patients to go home. One of them was a boy, who had recently fallen from a tree and ruptured his spleen. Due to chronic malaria, the spleen grew huge and accreted with his large liver. Despite a huge incision, I could not see behind the ribs, and at the same time I could not extend the cut up to the thorax – I had to run part of the operation only by touch.

While leaving the surgical ward, I can see some patients sitting on a long wooden bench underneath the veranda. They are waiting for new bandages. "Please don't forget to get them new bandages," I remind Goum. "Sure, of course, but except for that one..." and he points to the end of the bench – there are two little black boys sitting. The four-year old has a bandage on his neck, the other is about nine years old. The flabby, dirty, and ripped clothes make them look very poor right at first glance. They both smile at me roguishly. "They brought nothing with them, neither bandages, nor gauze squares," complains the head of the ward. "Moreover, they claim they came to see you." "That's right." I sweep my hand, "I know both of them. It's the young Paterne with his brother; they live in the neighborhood underneath the mission. They know what they are doing, they are actually my ‚private' patients."

I remember that about a week ago, when I was just finishing my lunch, the watchman Saco approached me and told me I had a visit. The two tots were waiting for me at the gate. The elder was holding the little one's hand, and as he saw me coming, he declared: "Mbih gah ti bah moh, docteur – I came to see you, doctor." "Ngbagah, ti nie? – And why?" I wondered. "A suku lakweh, lakweh – he's got it all swollen, constantly," the older boy explained, pointing at his younger brother's neck. Yes, there really was a huge lump at the front of Paterne's neck, an innate cyst of about an inch and a half in diameter. Something didn't seem right, so I asked him again. "Wait, and where's your father?" "On the road", the boy replied. "And mother?" "On the field." Replied the tot again, patiently. "So who sent you to me?" I asked, in search of an explanation. The boy merely shook his head, meaning "nobody", and then he pushed his sibling before him, and repeated his plea again. "A suku lakweh, lakweh – He's got it all swollen, constantly." I realized then what was going on. The elder brother, taking care of his sibling in his parent's absence, thought the parent's kept ignoring Paterne's condition, so he decided to assume responsibility for the situation himself. "Well, I am sorry, but you need to tell your mother to come to see me after work," I ended my dialogue with the boys. An elderly woman dropped by the very same evening. She hovered by the door, her eyes fixed on the ground, not knowing how to begin. It became clear, she had been aware of her son's problem, but she had neither the money for the operation, nor the bandages. That's why she didn't find the courage to enter the hospital. She was happy to hear I would operate on her boy for free, and give him the few bandages from my own supplies. So it happened. I removed little Paterne's cyst, and his brother now took him to the hospital for a new bandage. The boys are a perfect example of small African kids, who are growing up – for the most part – on the streets, and manage to take care of themselves.

The parents of a little boy approach me, while I am heading to the internal ward. He fell from a mango tree and broke his arm. "No food, no drinks," I say to his parents. "I must put him to sleep to straighten up the fracture."

I know how the sweet fruit appeals to the children, they climb the trees and sometimes they fall down. The hospital nurses – there are more men than women working as medical personnel in Africa – call this the "mango tree syndrome".

Many of the local injuries are of similar nature; they occur during fruit crops, work in the fields, and rarely in brawls or duels. The complicated, more severe injuries – that arise from car accidents for instance, which European surgeons are well acquainted with – are very rare here. There are about twenty cars in the city of 17,000 people!

In normal circumstances I would tend to the fracture immediately, today however, as I am the only one to see to the hospital, I must postpone it for a while.

It is my duty to decide about their further treatment of the hospitalized patients. And with the exception of ultrasound and surgery – everything is taken care of by the nurses.

So when a patient comes to the hospital, they are examined and treated by a nurse. I only see them, when their heath calls for hospitalization, or when the nurse needs some advice. I am also not called out for ordinary births. The doctor is sent for only when things don't proceed the way they should, and a caesarian section is to be carried out, or when there is a severe complication to be dealt with.

Basically, the nurses here do the job of the younger doctors back home. Their professional qualities vary, but most of them – thanks to their everyday practice and effort – have obtained such experience and knowledge that they greatly outdo the nurses back home. There is a problem, however: the local medical personnel – just like in other hospitals in the county – has been receiving no salary from the state for the past few months. Nonfunctional administration and the empty treasury make it simply impossible to pay these people. Everyone is still waiting for better times to come. This, of course, subscribes to the professional morale of the hospital staff, and their "economic" approach to the patients.

For me, this means facing a daily struggle with the nurses against prescribing medicine the patients don't really need; it's sole purpose thus being the growth of funds in the hospital pharmacy. This means that only the well-to-do patients may afford the treatment, and even they often interrupt the treatment due to the lack of finances. That's why I try to make sure on my daily round whether the patients get only what they really need.

8.30am

I am entering the internal ward, being already expected by my colleagues. Just like in the surgical ward, we greet one another and shake hands. A new round starts.

The illnesses I encounter here are rather different from those we come across in Europe. Here we treat patients with TBC, malaria, liver cirrhosis, but mostly with AIDS. When I first came to the hospital, I was shocked at how quickly this illness was spreading in Africa. In the years of my previous work in European hospitals I had seen much less of these cases than I did during my first three weeks here. Unfortunately, even this pokey corner in the middle of Africa isn't spared by the epidemic. AIDS has been growing strong here. My estimate is that about 15% of the Bozoum population is HIV positive.

Among the hospitalized, there is also a young girl, of about 22. Her father is one of the nurses. He is desperate, knowing that she has just a few months left to live. This illness, together with malaria, accounts for most of the deaths in our hospital. Unfortunately, there is a lack of public education that would perhaps change the conduct of the Central Africans. Any mention of AIDS is pointless. According to a number of natives, this is a mere invention of the whites. Talking of AIDS here is a taboo.

8.40am

I quickly walk through the maternity ward. There are only two mothers – they gave birth today, without any complications. "Doctor, doctor, none of them has paid for the hospitalization!" Regine, the birth assistant, reports indignantly. I can only shrug my shoulders. "They have no funds, I guess they have spent their last money to buy clothing for their babies." I know, that although the parents are mostly very poor, they somehow always manage to obtain the basic clothes for their offspring.

Money is a constant problem here. There is no social security, and there is no health insurance in the country. When somebody turns sick, they must pay the full cost of the whole kit and caboodle. And when the patient is hospitalized, they must pay the hospitalization fee, and very often the operation too.

I take a look at the newborns. Their white skin reminds me of European kids. It is within the next few days that, under the

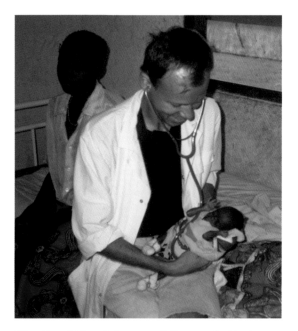

The first kid weighs over 5.5 pounds. Rather chubby, by African standards!

influence of the African sun their bodies begin to create the black pigment.

The first kid weighs over 5.5 pounds. Rather chubby, by African standards! The other child is doing worse. It came into world prematurely. His mother was ill during the pregnancy, so it's not only small, but also thin. Being only 3.3,it looks like a little monkey. In its overly huge dress, big hat and socks it's particularly cute. "Stuff his dress well with fluffs of cotton," I advise the parents; it's no problem for them to obtain cotton. There is cotton everywhere. Many of the locals grow it in their fields. "And you, please prepare our incubator for him," I turn to Regina. Straight away she asks the relatives to warm up water on the fireplace, then she pours the steaming water into two PET lemonade bottles. She coats them with tatters, so the baby won't get burned, and then she lays the baby carefully between them. Eventually, she wraps both the bottles and the baby with a stretch of colorful African cloth – "pagne", for the baby to be protected from the coldness of the African night. This shrimp has a fair chance to make it. Thanks to its developed sucking reflex, we need no stomach probe.

Until recently, I wouldn't ever believe that kids could ever survive in such poor conditions, but these small, resilient little African children have confirmed the opposite. I believe this one will make it, too.

9am

It's 9am. I still have to go to the pediatrics ward – the most occupied ward of the hospital. A small boy I recently operated on for a stomach abscess keeps watch for me. He is to be released today. He smiles at me, and offers me the donut his father bought for him a while ago.

And here comes Semplice, the head of the pediatrics ward. Again we repeat the indispensable procedure of shaking hands. "Marie died in the morning," he gives me the sad news. Although one could expect this to happen on a daily basis, I feel shaken by her death; I had grown to like the little girl.

The eight-year-old Marie has been in our hospital for a couple of months, sick with a severe lung and stomach form of tuberculosis. Despite all our efforts, her health gradually grew worse. Finally she could hardly eat or breathe, and yet I can't recall hearing her complain. Every morning, during the rounds, her pleasant smile would welcome me, and she would answer my questions only with "Yakapeh – I am fine." She didn't have the strength to stand up in the last days, but she kept her smile. Most of the African patients are like her: patient, modest and grateful for any small help.

I feel shaken, and sad as I leave with Semplice for the rounds. We enter two small rooms, where about 15 sick children are squeezed together with their mothers and other relatives. "Ala sighighi – Get out!" cries Semplice, vigorously making all the relatives leave the room. He wants every round to run in absolute quiet.

I cannot miss a four-year-old girl who is watching me from one corner. It's the girl I operated on during the night. She had fallen from a tree yesterday morning, piercing her stomach and large intestine with a root of the tree. Her desperate and totally exhausted parents brought her on their back, walking 25 miles from their village. "Tonga nah nie – How's it going?" I ask in a friendly tone. "Nzalah a salah mbih – I am hungry," the girl silently complains, lowering her eyes. "Unfortunately, I can't give you food today, but I'm happy you are feeling better."

I stop by the little bed of a four-year-old girl, the daughter of a local police officer. She won't even look at me! She is in a sulk. Recently, I punctured with a colleague festering exudates in her chest. She fought back, as hard as she could, screaming shrilly and repeating desperately:" Mbih gweh ti tehneh nah papa – I gonna tell my father, I gonna tell my father!" as if he would put us in prison because of this. Fortunately, she didn't succeed in persuading him. The only option left is to scowl at me.

Quickly I go over the other children, checking up on their medicine and – as usual – some are left without it. Their parents simply don't have the money. I'll look for any surplus medicines in the mission storeroom, as soon as I am through with the round.

10.15am

After 10 I get inside my Citroën, and quickly leave for the storeroom. I am in a rush. Today I am going to operate the inguinal hernia.

"Nzalah a salah mbih – I am hungry," the girl silently complains, lowering her eyes. (Page 87)

Soon I am going through the medication which missionaries get from their friends and Italian sponsors. There are also a few boxes I obtained before my departure to Africa. There is medical material including medicine from Switzerland, France and Prague. Put together, this means a solid stock of medicine, syringes, needles, infusion sets, gloves and other material. It's due to these gifts only, that I have the possibility to help those, who can't afford to pay their treatment. All patients, of course, make themselves look the poorest of the poorest, but – as the mission medical supplies are not bottomless – it's up to me to decide, whom to give the medical means, and whom not. It's the poor clothes that often help, and the deportment of the patient and the family. The best piece of advice, however, I get from the nurses who are well acquainted with the financial conditions of their neighbors. Other patients, unfortunately, must buy their medicine themselves. This is because the hospital's only income derives from medicine sales. Without it, the hospital would cease to exist. It hasn't received any support from the State for some time already, and this puts me in a situation in which I must both strive to provide enough medicine for everyone in need, and – at the same time – I cannot inhibit the medicine business that keeps the whole hospital going. I also have to keep track of what medicine and medical material we are running out of in the hospital pharmacy. In Europe, when there is a shortage of certain medicine, it's not a problem to procure it at the local seller. Not here. Both medicine, and medical material such as bandages and catheters have to be bought months in advance. There are times, when these are unattainable even in the capital city. The golden rule in Africa is: save everything that is not yet lacking.

I remember a story that happened in the beginning of February, shortly after my arrival in Bozoum. Goum asked me to help him out with a certain problem. One patient in the surgical ward had a bladder catheter inserted that was impossible to remove. Most probably the thin duct that empties the balloon got clogged, and that kept holding the catheter in the bladder. I asked Goum for scissors, and with a choreographed motion, I cut the catheter in the middle. Thus I cleared away the obstruction, the balloon deflated, and I could then easily remove the catheter. It's a standard European solution. Goum, however, stared at me aghast, moaning: "Such damage! Until you came, there were two

Fortunately, the boxes with medical material arrived from Europe
shortly after.

catheters in the hospital! We would sterilize them, so we could
use them repeatedly. But now! We have only one left! You
damaged a very precious thing, mister!" Fortunately, the boxes
with medical material arrived from Europe shortly after, so I
could rectify the "irreparable damage".

10.45am

As I am returning with medicine to the hospital, the birth
assistant dashes in. "Doctor, a woman was brought in, she has
been giving birth since yesterday." Immediately I run to examine
her. The situation is clear. The woman has a narrow pelvis. A
caesarian section must be performed without delay.

Thus I am forced to put off the reposition of the kid's broken
arm, and the hernia operation.

"Kangah beh ti moh – Be strong, it'll be all right," I try to cheer the young mother. I grasp a scalpel in my hand, and with a local anesthetic I quickly open the belly and the uterus. When I take out the neonate, Goum injects anesthetic into her arm. For the rest of the operation, she will be asleep. I didn't have the

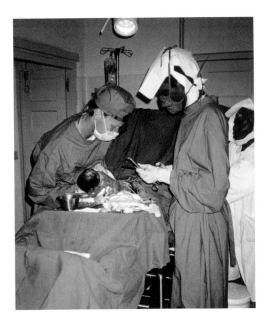

The woman could finally have her first baby. She had lost six children during her previous births. (page 92)

luxury of making her sleep from the beginning. There is no option of artificial lung respiration in the hospital, and I couldn't take the risk of the mother vomiting in her sleep – while I would be taking out the baby – or the child having respiration problems due to the given anesthetics. Luckily, the operation ran without complications. The woman could finally have her first baby. She had lost six children during the previous births. This was a last minute call, but still in time.

Right after the operation, I leave to take an x-ray of the kid's arm; he has been waiting since early morning. The x-ray is the hospital's hot news. It was quite a stroke of luck. Sometime ago I met Mr. Buhl, the most influential man in the region. He's the head of the developing program DROP that – financed by the German government – deals with the building of roads and renovation of hospitals. That day he sent his driver to tell me he was feeling very sick. I diagnosed gall bladder colic, caused by a stone, and told him my prognosis. Being well acquainted with local conditions, he flew to Europe the very next day. They found the stone, and removed it, and he then – out of gratefulness – promised to help with the installation of an x-ray machine. He also offered to help replenish other hospital equipment. In the beginning, I was thinking of only about three surgical instruments, but eventually I ordered from Germany about fifty various things (Humby's Dermatome, a set for trans-osseous traction, dentist's forceps) about 16,000 Euro in total. Mr. Buhl kept his word, so Bozoum ranks now as one of the country's best-equipped hospitals.

The x-ray indicated a rare sort of elbow fracture. I'm not a specialist in child traumatology, and never before had I executed a reposition of such a fracture. Unfortunately, the nearest child surgical ward is in Bangui, 280 miles from here. It's more than clear the parents can afford neither the trip, nor the treatment in the capital city. The troublesome situation must be dealt with somehow. In the operation hall, I open my surgery textbook, and follow it now step by step, as if it was a cookbook. The reposition turns out well.

1pm

At 1pm, I finally get to operate on the hernia. Until recently, this kind of operation was hardly attainable for the poorer population. It was after my arrival to the hospital, that this operation could be executed with only local anesthesia. This method both lowered the price of the operation to 40% of its original price, and cut down the high risks the patients in general anesthesia were facing. Such operations are always hazardous due to insufficient hospital equipment, both for the patient and the doctor.

I will never forget a nine-month old boy I operated on for his inborn defect in the navel region. Since there was no respirator available at the hospital, I didn't have any way to secure his airways by a tracheal pipe as back in Europe. I also wasn't aware his mother had breastfed him before the surgery. The baby began to vomit in his sleep during the operation, inhaled its vomit and stopped breathing. This was a desperate moment. The child didn't breathe and I was dumbfounded. I stood, all in sterile clothing, facing his open stomach. What next? Only seconds separated the child from death. Quickly I grasped the boy's legs, and lifted him to the ceiling. Total chaos ensued. The sterile instruments fell to the floor, intestines prolapsed from the cut, and the sterile surgery turned at once non-sterile.

Suddenly his airway was freed and he coughed. Goum immediately cleansed his stomach with a tampon, and I had new instruments brought in. I administered a sterile rinse on the intestines, and completed the not-quite-germfree operation. The only thing left was to give the child some antibiotics, and then I could only pray for him not to develop an inflammation in his lungs or belly. Everything turned out well, thank god. The next week I removed the sutures and allowed the child home. The boy was exceptionally lucky, and so was I. In Africa, if a patient dies in the hospital, magic is at fault. The relatives blame neither the doctor, nor the nurses. However, when the patient dies during surgery, it is always the doctor's fault.

The hernia operation runs smoothly. The patient is awake; he just does not sense the cut. I feel calm. I know the surgery is much less dangerous, than if we had put him to sleep. At the hospital table – there is no air conditioning, of course – the temperature has reached 92 F. I feel horribly warm, all dressed in a thick, hermetic cloak, a cap, and a mouthpiece. Every once in a while Goum mops the drops of sweat trickling down my forehead. Although I feel terribly thirsty, I must finish the surgery first. "And now the last stitch, and – finished" I rejoice. "Awe – finished," my assistant Albert breathes with relief. He, too, has had a hard day today, and he's looking forward to the afternoon siesta. "You can eat and drink what you feel like," I say to the patient who is putting on his clothes already. "Goum will take you to your room."

2.45pm

I get back home before 3pm. Everyone at the mission has had lunch by then. I have my meal kept in the kitchen, thank god. Marcello passes by. He always has the feeling I don't eat enough. "Eat, eat, or Africa is going to eat you!" He prods me with a smile. After lunch I take a little rest: I want to go to the small village of Konkeré, about 25 miles from Bozoum, where Sebastian is to celebrate a Mass. It's a good change of scenery. At least I will free myself from the bustle of hospital events, and get more acquainted with life in the bush.

3.30pm

"Get ready for take off", Sebastian cries, "and bring some water with you." I quickly fill the tank with filtered water, rushing for the small terrain truck, where he is waiting for me with Marina, a mirthful Uruguay nun, who joins us. Soon we are driving on a clay road, heading north. Clouds of red dust tower behind the car, and there is high burnt grass and low twisted shanks of bushy shrubs surrounding us. Sometimes I can see the stripes of smoke from all the frequent fires rising to the sky. A few birds of prey keep orbiting above us. They hunt for small beasts, deserting the fires.

He is waiting for me with Marina,
a mirthful Uruguay nun, who joins us.

The journey doesn't take too long. We are already expected. Sebastian's hearing confessions, and the local choir is rehearsing a few songs. Marina is preparing the altar, and organizes the children's meeting from the "aitah kweh" community. I take a short walk. The village seems like those I already know. Little clay houses with hay roofs and small, glassless windows, coops standing on high posts, fireplaces at the door, small goats and hogs. Soon I return to the chapel. I want to do some singing with the children. They are definitely the sweetest of the population. They are constantly smiling and cheerful, and they are thrilled by

Children are definitely the sweetest of the population.

the tiniest trifle. Among the local missionaries, I am the only one with blond hair and blue eyes, so I am a great spectacle for them. They always turn after me; the smallest and most curious ones come over to take a closer look.

4.30pm

The Mass proceeds in a very joyful air. In the bush villages, it's celebrated only every few weeks. They wait for their turn. That's why today's Mass is such an event for the locals. Wildly they beat their drums, dance and sing. I come and join them.

5.45pm

The Celebratory Mass ends. As we leave the church, the setting sun tints everything red. The village women light up their fires and cook dinner. One man invites us for a visit. It's impossible to decline.

We enter a low house lumped out of clay. A single kerosene lamp lights the dwelling. On the compacted earth, there lie a few mats. In the middle of the room, on a small rough-hewn table lies the dinner; a ball of manioc and bits of boiled chicken meat with vegetable sauce. It's the traditional celebratory meal of the natives. The host brings a jar with water to wash our hands. One eats with one's hands. Marina shows me the way to pinch off the mutual ball of manioc and dip it in the sauce. Suddenly I remember my lectures from parasitology, and the guidebook warnings. Well, too late, it's better not to think about it... "Ah nzereh mingih – It's very good," we praise the food. But nobody finishes it, we all know the host gives out, but he is very poor. Soon we take leave. The last handshakes, and then we return to Bozoum. For some time I can still hear our friends crying: "Ala langoh nzonih – Be well!"

6.15pm

We leave the village in the dark. The Toyota is shaking, and waggling on the stony road. "There is a sick kid in a nearby village. You will take a look at him, won't you?" asks Marina. I nod.

We pull up at a cluster of huts, keeping the lights on. A well-built man gets out from one them, carrying a baby wrapped in rags. I have nothing on me. No stethoscope, no thermometer. I take the kid into my arms, pressing him close to my ears, and listen to his breathing. After a few months of my stay in the country, where there is a lack of almost everything, I learned to make a do only with my senses. After a while I turn to the father: "It's going to be all right, but you must go with us to the mission to grab some medicine." The man agrees, and climbs on the bumper of the car. He walks back home the very same night with the medicine in his pocket.

7.50pm

After a common meal at the mission, I leave for the hospital to check up on the patients I operated on today. The lights are turned off already. For two months there is no public light in Bozoum, except in the little house, where the night service burns a weak kerosene lamp. Still, one can see. A full moon illuminates the whole yard, reflected by the metal roofs of the pavilions. Huge mango treetops tower darkly against the clear sky. There is silence everywhere.

I enter the surgical ward. "Baralah kweh – Hello everyone!" I turn to the silhouettes lying on the ground. They are the relatives of the sick. "Barah minghi, minghi, mon docteur – Hello, hello, doctor," one can hear from all corners. I can find my patients easily despite the darkness. With a flashlight in my hand, I check up on their wounds, and their general health. The woman who underwent the c-section has already awoken from her anesthetic slumber. Her newborn is lying next to her, wrapped in a stretch of cloth. "What name did you give her?" I ask the parents. Instead of an answer, they surprise me with a question. "And what is your name, doctor?" "Marcel," I reply with a smile. "Her name be Marcelline, then." So there is one more little Marcella in Africa.

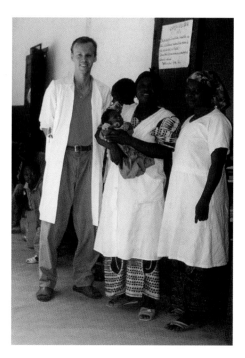

"Her name is Marcelline, then."

The patient after the hernia surgery, and the kid with the broken arm are ok as well. I can calmly go to sleep. Slowly I return to the mission. The moon shines brightly on my way. Singing and tom-toms come from the city in the valley below. So again, an African day comes to a close.

Chapter Twelve

The Mysterious Africa

"So they take me for a magician," I say in a by-the-way tone during our lunch. "How come?" Marcello lowers his spoon, staring at me closely. I notice that his smile has vanished from his face. "Well, it was so," I explain, "Yesterday afternoon I dropped by the playground in front of the mission. Sister Marina was organized the "Aitah – kweh", an afternoon full of entertainment for the smallest children. The little boys danced, sang and played various games. I wanted to have some fun, too, so I showed them a few simple tricks with matches. Today during the rounds, one woman suddenly asked me: "Doctor, I heard you do magic? My son told me. He saw you yesterday at the playground."

"Hmm," Marcello seems unusually serious, "can I tell you something? Don't do such things here. You are in Africa, and people here really believe in magic. For the small children your tricks weren't just tricks, but a true instance of magic." I suddenly realize that although the kids liked my tricks, they didn't really wonder that much, and they didn't try to find out the how I performed the tricks.

"It wouldn't do any good, if you gained the reputation of a magician," Marcello continues. "It's a dangerous thing here. 80% of all lawsuits deal with the accusation of sorcery. The local legal system distinguishes and recognizes the notion of sorcerers and sorcery. When a child, or a young person dies, or there is a natural disaster, poor crop, or a disease, the natives will accept your explanation e.g. that it was a parasite causing malaria that killed the baby, but he won't content himself with this. He will search for the person, who sent the parasite on the baby, and he is going to call for revenge."

In the hospital, I would often encounter the African principle of ‚searching for the cause'. Everything has its order in Africa. Chance does not exist. Whatever deviates from the norm, demands an explanation. A good example of this could be the relatively frequent disease – meningitis. The symptoms of the initial phase are fever and neurological indications. The Central Africans believe that during this phase the distant sorcerer causes the soul of the baby to gradually turn into an animal soul. As soon as the baby loses consciousness, the transition is complete. After that the soul of the baby – now as the soul of the antelope or some other animal, wanders about the bush. When the child dies, the explanation is clear: Some hunter shot the animal. The Sorcerer is the source of all the evil. He works always in secret and masks himself: his behavior in public doesn't differ from other people. One must unveil him. Suspicion from three people is enough to launch a lawsuit. The accused may be some very able individual, who has been doing exceptionally well recently, or someone in dispute with the injured. Africans take the law into their own hands. In larger towns, the accused ends up in prison, in the villages he gets lynched. The State and the missionaries fight lynching as much as they can; yet these sad events still occur sometimes. In most cases, envy or a personal dispute looms behind the accusation. If the wrongly accused manages to get off with only a beating, he can talk of fortune. Lynching often ends with death, and the house of the accused reduced to ashes.

"How's that possible," I wonder, "the majority of people in Bozoum are Christian, the churches are always full on Sundays…" Marcello just nods his head: "Well, you're right about that, most people here are Christian, and in truth regard Christianity as their faith. Conversely, they uphold a set of traditional beliefs they consider in no clash with the former. See, try to ask some of them about Mamiota, the water nymph."

A few days later, I was sitting in a hospital office with the head nurse of the internal ward, discussing the treatment of some patients. I asked then: "Apropos, Jean-Paul, does Mamiota live in the stream under the mission?" "Of course not," he shook his head. "I guess it isn't too hot with the traditional beliefs anymore" I said to myself, disappointed. But Jean-Paul surprised me straight away: "The fathers from the mission couldn't stand her in the neighborhood, so they drove her out a few years ago. Every little child knows this." I could hardly believe my ears: the medical personnel constitute the most educated class in town. "I don't know anything about it," I bade him to speak more. "Mamiota is the water nymph, she resembles a beautiful, fair woman, and now she dwells in the Ouham River, about 2 miles west of Bozoum. She reveals herself to the one, who happens to come to her dwelling place exactly at midnight. Once you see her, she takes possession of your heart. Enchanted, You follow her to the river, and at night she comes to your home. With her magic, she starts to fulfill your wishes, but soon she will ask for a sacrifice: she wants your parents, your brothers and finally, she takes hold of you, too." "You were saying she was a beautiful, fair woman? Well, that really sounds interesting, for a white man like me. I guess I will go and take a look at her." "No, no, no," I hear somebody's cry from behind. I turned around and there was another nurse standing at the door. "You can't do that, doctor, we need you here!" He warned me, with horror in his eyes. I didn't want to disturb them anymore, so I returned to the subject of patients' treatment. I realized, that magic and sorcery are still a serious matter in Africa, and I wouldn't try to perform my tricks in public again.

I remember the case of a youth of twenty-five, who was brought to the hospital. He was in a coma. Nurses told me that his rich old father owned a herd of cows. The son was unhappy seeing that the father didn't want to die, and the inheritance was still in the distance. So he searched for a sorcerer, and ordered his father's death. What he had ordered also happened. His father died, and he inherited the entire fortune. When he was digging the grave, he grazed the casket with his pickaxe. Since that very moment he began to feel ill. He died in the hospital the same day. Despite rapid examinations, we couldn't find out what had really happened. It seemed like an acute liver failure to me. This suggests a possible poisoning. I don't know, perhaps he had a younger brother, who... Or was there something mysterious, something inexplicable for us?

I never ran into a sorcerer in person during my African stay, but I had the chance once to examine the objects the sorcerers use while performing black magic. It was just about my sixth month in Africa, I was driving through the town of Berberati, situated at the edge of the rainforest, south of Bozoum. In the mission, I met an old Franciscan Father Humberto, one of the oldest missionaries in the country. He came to the Central African Republic fifty years ago. For a long time, he was working in the north, in the mountains of neighboring Chad, where the Panna tribe lives. As a priest, he would spend all his free time with the natives, and he also gradually earned their trust. So he had the chance to learn a great deal about the local customs and penetrate into their thinking. He knows much more about the locals than many European researchers who would often stay in Africa just for a few weeks or months.

Apart from his missionary vocation, for decades he devoted himself to his hobby, which is ethnography. For countless years he has been collecting and recording the narratives of patriarchs from different villages, comparing them together, and using them to base his study describing the outset of colonization in the northern regions in the beginning of the 20th century. It's a very interesting read, partially also because it's put together from the authentic narratives of eye witnesses. Other mentions of the historical period can be found in the accounts of French colonial officers. These, however, could hardly be regarded as objective.

Apart from recording the oral narratives of the locals, father Humberto also collects various indigenous objects. During the fifty years, he managed to assemble a unique collection of weapons, folk jewelry, torsos of clothing, masks, former currency, etc. These interesting things are now placed in the Missionary Museum in Yolé close to Bouar.

During my visit I told him I knew of his hobby from other missionaries, and I also praised his collection I had a chance to examine in Yolé sometime ago.

"If it interests you, I can show you another part of the collection –" he suggested, "– the part which is not open to the public." And he eagerly led me right away to the mission yard, where he unlocked a huge metal container. Just the type used for transportation in ships and trucks. It's interior with its exhibits reminded me of a miniature museum.

The old missionary looked over his unique collection, and then he pointed at the objects. "These are the tools of the African sorcerer." I was surprised at what a variety of things he had there. One by one, he took the items in his hand, telling me stories about them: Let's take this stone bowl. It was used to prepare poisons. God knows how many deaths its responsible for. Or this stone – you see, there are three heads carved in the corners. The sorcerer placed it at the crossroad in his village, and the heads tracked where everybody came and went. The sorcerer would come for the report now and then. Because of this information he collected about his tribe, nothing could ever escape him."

Just as interesting are the weird figures with a beak instead of a nose. "These statues portray the bad spirit called "likundu", the

Franciscan explained. "You could bring them to life at night, and they would follow all your orders." Then he grabbed another mysterious statue, as if carved from stone. "The sorcerer would bury this statue by a hut to stop the growth of the child who lived there." And so, Humberto initiated me into many of the mysteries. Then he looked over the remaining sinister statues, and picked up one more: "This one caused the mother to give birth to a disfigured child. As you can see, the sorcerers would use only very useful and practical things," the priest ended his talk with a grin.

I grab some of the other things, examining them closely from all sides. "This must be really old stuff, I guess the natives don't believe in such things any longer," I say with a questioning look at father Humberto. "Well, you're wrong, I tell you nothing has changed in Africa in this regard." When we close the container, I am quite happy Humberto has these things locked up safe and sound.

Another traditional figure of African society is the healer (gerisseur). From the societal point of view, he is less dangerous than the sorcerer. He is not the cause of misfortune and disease; conversely, he is the one who tries to cure them. In most cases, he is usually the first person the native approaches. Only when the sickness doesn't recede, will the sick person set out for the hospital. That's his last hope. The only remaining outcome after that is death. Unfortunately, this detainment by the healer, and the lack of finances often cause the patient to come to the hospital too late.

I still vividly remember one man with severe burns sitting tight at home for a whole month, until the infection virtually decomposed his arm. The only solution left was amputation.

Many times I saw women who were giving birth at home, and then came to the hospital a day or two later, when the child was already dead. It cost us much effort then to even save the mother. I would often face the outcomes of the traditional treatment in my daily work. Most common was scarification, i.e. multiple short cuts at the spot where the patient felt pain. I would often make use of these scars in my diagnosis. For example, when I discovered multiple scarifications in the lower abdomen, chronic pelvis infection was usually the case. When I saw a man with numerous scars on the hip and lower part of the chest, I could guess pneumonia and the pleura infection. By the Moslem nomads of the M'Bororo tribe I would often – instead of cuts – notice round burns caused by heated cow horns. Many children on the pediatrics ward wore around their hips or ankles slim lather straps with "kri-kri" – tiny amulets against evil spirits. I must say, however, that the hospital personnel would in most cases keep a distance from such practices.

Once it happened that a nurse (securiste) from a nearby village broke his leg at the thigh. Securiste is somebody with a minor amount of training in the field curing simple illnesses in his village, but he should – first of all – forward the more serious cases to the hospital. The work probably doesn't pay much, so he decided to try his luck as a prospector. He had bad luck. He was caught in a cave-in during one of his excavations. After being rescued his family brought him to the hospital in the morning. Because I was just going to operate on a patient, I just quickly examined the man, saying: "we will do something with it." When I returned from the operating room, he was gone. It seemed strange, so I asked my colleagues to find out what had happened. The next day I ran into an irritated Goum: "For some reason he thought we wanted to cut his leg off," he explained, "and he was also short of money. His relatives consigned him to the cure of a marabu – a Moslem healer. He put healing leaves on his leg, and fixed it with a splint." After saying this, Goum just shook his head in disbelief, and gave me a questioning look. "I don't think this is good," I said discontented, "his leg will mend in the wrong position, and it will be permanently shorter." "I know," the head of the surgical ward agreed, "and he is our colleague, basically. We can't leave him this way." "But what makes you think the marabu will let his client go?" I argued. My colleague thought for a moment, and then he said: "You can leave this to me." Securiste was back in the hospital the very next day. "How did you manage?" I asked Goum in surprise. He laughed: "It was easy. We went to the marabu and told him we didn't have the slightest intention of having the patient back, and that we were thankful that the marabu would now be covering the expenses of 60,000 CFA (Central African Franks, about $150 US) the state had invested in the nurse's professional training. It's evident, that the nurse could neither walk, nor work with a shorter leg. The marabu himself then talked the family into bringing the sick man back to the hospital, he wouldn't have anything to do with him anymore."

We laughed with Goum: it was clear how confident the marabu was about his abilities as a healer. Neither have I ever heard anything about the expenses invested by the state into the training of a nurse.

However, not all of my encounters with healers' activities had happy endings. One day, a woman in a coma was brought into the hospital. The family was well off, and paid for a single room. My examination showed that she was sick with meningitis. After three days of my treatment her health rapidly improved: she gradually came around, began to eat, speak, and she even sat once. I was happy, because this was a real success. My hope that she would heal proved premature, however. The fourth day I found her dead. I couldn't believe it. Soon I received the explanation. The treatment seemed for the family too long, so one evening they secretly brought a healer to the bed of the sick. This was easily done, she was isolated in a single room, and no one took notice. This proved fatal. The healer and his medicaments managed to do away with the almost healthy patient in thirty minutes. The hurriedly called nurses couldn't save the situation. I am not saying the healer intended her death; perhaps it was the reaction of "my" antibiotics and his – for me entirely unknown – herbal drugs. It's hard to hit upon a clear explanation in such cases.

Old myths are still alive in black Africa, with sorcery and healers lurking on your every step.

Chapter Thirteen

Natives' Diet

"Gerome, I don't mind manioc at all, but it makes me wonder that you can eat it every day," I turn to our cook, taking the last piece from the bowl, and dipping it – in African style – into the vegetable sauce. Manioc is traditionally served in the form of "boules", a ball of oozy dough, and consists mainly of pure starch. The meal is substantial as far as the calories go, but it totally lacks any taste, and without sauce, it's virtually inedible for a European. Gerome just shakes his head, uncomprehendingly. "But we could never do without manioc. It's the foundation of our cuisine." "And what do you eat back home?" he asks me after a short break of silence. "Mainly potatoes," I confess. The cook bursts into laughter, and laughs so hard that tears are rolling down his eyes. "Oh, you are so weird," he says, as he cleans up the table. I think I can understand. There are, of course, potatoes even in Central Africa, and the Africans sometimes grow them in their gardens, but they use it exclusively as a part of the vegetable side dish, just like we use salad, peppers, or tomatoes back home. Manioc, that is something different. It is the main dish here, and the natives love it. And if you serve it to any visitor, no one will feel offended, you can be sure about that.

Women eventually crush manioc
in mortars before cooking.

So wherever you travel in Africa, you always find fields of these manioc bushes with peculiarly ragged leaves from which the natives prepare the vegetable sauces. But it is the roots that are most important for the natives. Two years after the planting, the bush is dug up, and the roots – reminiscent of huge parsley – are washed, chopped into smaller pieces and then plunged for 48 hours into water to soak out the poisonous cyanides. The roots are then chopped into small knobs of about an inch each. After that they are dried under the sun on flat stones along the roads and in just about everyplace imaginable. The sweet smell of

Then the whole family goes to work in the fields.

drying manioc roots is present in all inhabited regions. Bags of white, dried lumps are then sold at the market, women eventually crush manioc in mortars before cooking.

"Gerome, how often do you actually eat?" I ask the cook again, who is now about to take a break. "Usually we have only one really big meal – in the evening." Gerome, who works at the mission for one day a week, nods his head: "In the morning I usually just have something to drink, or I just grab a little something to eat, and my whole family goes to work in the fields. We don't return home at noon, because the preparation of lunch and the journey there and back would take too long. As you can see, there is no time for food during the day, but only in the evening. Then there's time

I am happy I got to know Gerome. He is nice
and he is a good worker, too.

enough. My wife lights up the fire, and the whole family sits around it. We eat slowly, and tell each other what happened during the day. Sometimes our neighbors join us. That's how it goes." He gives me one last friendly smile, and then he disappears into the darkness.

I am happy I got to know Gerome. He is nice and he is a good worker, too. And since I don't really feel very confident in Sango, I am happy he also speaks French. I always learn something interesting about the life of the locals from him, and because he works at the mission as a cook, the underlying theme of our conversation is food. Now I know that except for manioc, fruit

They often enrich their diet with fish
from the nearby Ouham River.

and various vegetables, chicken meat also forms a part of the common diet. It's also easy to get. Apart from poultry, the Central Africans also keep hogs and goats. They often enrich their diet with fish from the nearby Ouham River, which is about the size of the Sázava River in the Czech Republic. Sometimes they draw out a fish the size of an adult man. Beef is the only thing the locals must buy at the market. Exclusively the nomadic M'Bororo sell this meat. They are the only people here who own huge herds of cows and know how to handle them.

Meat is really precious here, so even Gerome sets out for a hunt in the bush sometimes. He baits rodent traps, and sometimes he catches a bird or snake. Just like in other African countries, there are lots of large animals living here. They are protected, and one needs a special permit to hunt them. In the region where I am living, however, most of them have been virtually exterminated, with the exception of the elephants and hippos. Even they are hard to spot. The rainforests in the south, and the savannas in the northern and eastern regions of the Central African Republic are, on the contrary, full of animals. Their numbers and diversity are second to none among the famous safaris in eastern Africa.

My 'right hand' Albert, the head nurse of the hospital, comes from Nola, a small town in the middle of the forests in the southern part of the country. He grew up among people who – just like their ancestors centuries ago – set out into the forests to hunt and collect fruit. He has friends also among the local Pygmies who don't know agriculture at all, and live exclusively by hunting. Albert invited me repeatedly and told me that the locals – Pygmies especially – consider the rainforest their home and they don't listen to the authorities telling them what to hunt. They cope easily with large animals, too. Unlike poachers, however, they don't kill the animals in large numbers.Their bread and butter is mainly fruit, insects, caterpillars and fish. A crossbow with poisoned arrows helps them enrich their diet. Albert says they use it to hunt monkeys, above all. Nobody knows how this medieval weapon made it to the pygmies. It's a fact, however, they were using it before the arrival of the first whites.

The natives of Nola have developed a very unique method for hunting large snakes, constrictors, which dwell in large dens under the ground. The hunter first spreads thick peanut butter gruel over his leg up to the groin, then sticks it into a hole, and waits. Eventually the snake will come, and start swallowing his leg. Everybody knows this species of snake has the unique ability to open its jaws to such an extent, that it swallows its pray – rodents, for example – whole. The enzymes in its digestive tract then break it down. The peanut butter spread so serves as a reliable protection for the hunter's skin. It would take a snake several hours before it could reach thigh height. When I asked Albert what this felt like, he replied: "It gets a little warm, and it's pretty tight, but one can put up with it." The hunter then pulls out a sharp knife, sticks it in the corner of the snake's maw, and then rips it lengthwise, as if he were unraveling the seams of his pants. So he kills the snake without damaging its precious skin, which he can later sell profitably at the market.

The hunt for elephants in the rainforest I find very barbaric, too. The natives don't have rifles, and their spears are ineffective on elephants, so they have developed a different and more insidious method. They hammer long nails into a plank of wood, so the nails stick out dangerously at the other side. They bury these planks into the moldering leaves on the elephant trail. When the elephant steps on the nails, it thrusts with all of its weight, driving the nails deep into its foot. After this it can never hope to get rid of the plank. This causes it a lot of pain when walking, it moves less and less, cannot get enough food and gradually grows weaker. The hunters follow it, and when it cannot fight back anymore, they kill it with their spears.

Generally speaking, however, the classical hunting methods slowly vanish in Africa, and are still performed only in the small villages in the countryside and rainforests. People from the towns cannot hunt like this anymore.

The Central Africans don't hunt all of the local animals. The chameleon is a good example. It is considered a cursed animal, bringing only ill luck and misfortune. No one would ever come close to it, let alone eat it. Also, tradition forbids certain foods to women. A great deal of native women would ever touch snake meat, which is true also about the meat of the rocky goanna that is considered an exceptional delicacy among men. Once, when a colleague of mine invited us for dinner, Albert and I had the chance to taste goanna meat. "Why doesn't your wife join us?" I asked the host in surprise. "She doesn't want to," he said apologetically, "but I would let her, I don't believe the superstitions." After a while, he added: "Still, I understand the ban. The goanna meat is exceptionally delicious and it's also very rare. Men don't need to share it, at least."

Chapter Fourteen

The Blind Man

The sun was setting when I was leaving the hospital. It's one of the most beautiful moments of the African day. The burning sun, which has been glowing unmercifully right above our heads for the whole day, is now rapidly losing its intensity, and as it falls to the horizon, unexpected shadows begin to appear. The face of the landscape suddenly changes. The shadows grow longer and longer, and the sun disk – it seems now so much bigger – turns orange and crimson before it tints the hills around. Almost within reach, there dangles a huge, bloody orange from the sky. All of heaven and the hay roofs of the sheds, and the gray dry grass all around suddenly flare up in bright colors, which sharply contrast with the dark green hue of the mango trees and the protracting shadows.

Oblique, dazzling beams pierce into the car, and prevent me from driving fast. As I am straining my eyes and carefully watching the road, I notice the familiar silhouette of a man from the neighborhood, clumsily trying to chop down a small tree by the road.

"Oh my god, that can't be true!" I step on the breaks. I jump out of the car to make sure the figure belongs to the blind beggar. Now and then I meet him in the city – in the company of his two sons, five-year-olds, who are his virtual eyes and patiently guide him using a thin, metal stick. The blind man swings his axe in wide strokes, while the two little ones are jumping up and down right next to it. "Bah-bah, mo sale nieh – What are you doing, father?" I ask him, in shock, imagining how his children might wind up on my operation table, with one bad swing from his axe. "Kehkeh ti salah wah – Firewood," the blind man explains, with an innocent look on his face. "Baba, mo undah mweni koli – Father, you better ask someone else next time," I say with a serious tone, hoping to discourage him from such activities, and take the sharp axe from his hand. Then by a few strokes I fell the half-finished tree, its trunk being of soft wood. The whooping twins jump into the ditch, and drag the small tree out.

"Singitah nah moh, docteur – Thank you, doctor," the blind man cries, clasping his hands. "Nzapah a batah moh – God bless you!" I smile, and nod my head. I am glad it turned out well: the blind man has his wood, and I won't have to sew anybody together today.

Promptly, I get back into my car. As I am pulling out, I think of the situation of the handicapped back home and here in Africa. In Europe, there is a wide, functioning social network, where our "normal civilized society" places them. Various social and medical institutions thus substitute their families, and the handicapped are – as far as the material side is concerned – taken care of. In Africa, there are no such securities. When someone loses their sight, or an arm or a leg, or is physically or mentally handicapped, they can count on neither special considerations from the state, nor any financial or medical aid. The state is absolutely uncaring about how the people make a living. On the other hand, African society doesn't exclude them. They live normally among the members of their extended families, finding there the support and help they need. Although these poor people are often left with no other option but begging, they maintain a strong sense of family togetherness and solidarity. So now I am at a loss about who of the two is actually doing better.

Chapter Fifteen

On the Road

"Arrêtez – Stop!" Joseph cries out in alarm as he points at a battered Peugeot dashing from the left into the junction. I violently step on the breaks and let the car pass. "Why should I yield to cars coming from the left?" I ask my co-driver in wonder. "Because you are on a minor road," Joseph says, placidly again. "And can you tell me, how I should know this? There isn't any sign!" I say, irritated. Joseph has been employed at the mission for a number of years; he just moves on a bit and smiles: "There used to be one. It fell down one day, but that doesn't mean it isn't valid anymore. Everyone in Bangui knows this. "

So we are in the capital, driving on an asphalt road full of deep holes. Battered yellow cabs, and worn out Japanese and French cars snake deftly amongst them. The condition of these cars is quite alarming. One could say it's mostly heaps of wreckage running around. Cars lacking a fender here or there, or missing windows are no exception, let alone tires without tread. All cars are overloaded with goods and passengers; they fill in every vacant spot. Every once in a while, the glossy luxurious car of some rich owner will drive by, all spick and span. In the chaotic traffic, there is no shortage of carts, loaded to the top with bags of manioc, bananas, pineapples, and wood. Recurrently, there appear military jeeps with soldiers dressed in black. We can often see pedestrians hanging around in the middle of the street, just having a talk. Not even the horns disturb them. The air is thick with dust floating everywhere, and rhythmical African music reverberates from all corners.

Totally exasperated, I pull up on the side of the road. "Let's switch seats," I turn to Joseph in resignation, "this is horrible!" He knows his way around the capital, and he is good at dodging all the honking cars, potholes, barrows and people.

We are in a rush. We still have to stop at the bakery to buy a few bags of bread. It's the unwritten law for all who journey to the capital: only self-denial makes edible the sweet bread of Bozoum, and for no more than a limited period of time. I also must obtain at the pharmacy the shortage goods like plasters, bandages, cannulas, and scalpel blades. I wouldn't manage at the central pharmacy without the purchase order with the stamp of our hospital. The pharmacy is supplied chiefly by the international humanitarian organizations' aid to developing countries. These organizations (like IDA or MEDCOR) offer medical supplies at a much more favorable price than in Europe. This enables the local hospitals to take advantage of the price difference between buying and selling, which is the only profit they make. There is, however, a fixed maximum price for the medicaments that the hospitals cannot exceed. In order to prevent – at least partially – speculation buying of expensive medicaments, only representatives of medical facilities are allowed to shop at the pharmacy, that means no private customers.

It's going to take us a good hour to handle all of this. When I add another half an hour at the post office, where we need to get a few bags with mail for all of Bozoum, I estimate we won't make it out of the city before 10am. "What a trip!" I say with a sigh to Joseph, picturing us scorched by the midday heat. But he doesn't register me at all. He is busy driving, and attentively watching the market alongside the road. Then he rapidly stops. "Alah kuh mbih keteh, docteur – Just a moment, doctor!" He jumps out of the car, and rushes around to the back. I can see him in the rearview mirror arguing with an Arabian merchant. They debate and gesture with great animation. Soon Joseph returns empty-handed. "What's happening?" I ask. "Oh, I just spotted a really cute bed, it would be just perfect for my little daughter," Joseph replies. "So why didn't you buy it?" I wonder. Joseph merely shakes his head, saying foxily: "I just want to torment the Arab a bit, to lower the price. We are going to pull up here again, as soon as we are through with the pharmacy and the mail. "Oh no, so we won't leave the city before half past ten," I groan, knowing it always takes time before a deal is made in Africa.

Indeed, it's ten thirty-five when we finally leave the junction at PK 12, a fortified military station, which marks the city border. We still have about 280 miles to Bozoum. Hot air above the road is shimmering. We keep all the windows open, but it's still terribly hot inside the car. Sometimes I look back to make sure all the bags and boxes – including Joseph's new bed we laboriously fixed on the car roof – still hold.

In most cases, African roads go straight. One drives for a number of kilometers without a single turn. There are only a few exceptions. A terrain incline, about 45 miles from the capital is one of them: the road rises above the elevation of 600 ft for just a few miles. This section of the road has a very bad name among the local drivers. While we are driving through it, Joseph points at dozens of wrecks, grassy and rusty, they stick out to the sky from the shrubs of the bush like some weird monuments of ancient crashes.

At one point, we are facing a few trucks driving from the opposite direction. Joseph instantly drives to the very edge of the road, pulls up, and hurriedly closes all windows. He knows very well that the truck driver is very busy just driving through the curves, let alone paying consideration to a car coming from the opposite direction. Three Mercedes trucks from the 50s roll by, their bodies jammed with various commodities to the last inch. These mountains of goods, reaching five feet above the cabin roofs, are covered by tarps, fixed with string to the wooden paneling of the truck. On the flat peak of each of these trucks, about 16 ft high, there are between thirty and forty paying passengers. Just the idea of climbing up that high makes me dizzy. As the trucks pass by, clouds of dust roll over the car, and entirely block out our view. Now I finally understand Joseph's far-sighted action. It takes a while, before the dust settles and we roll on again.

"Listen, Joseph, let me tell you something." The encounter with the trucks reminded me of something that happened about a month ago. I was driving on the main road in downtown Bozoum, returning back to the mission. The night was pitch black, the moon hadn't come up yet, and the street lamps were out of order as usual. I drove very slowly, watching the road carefully. To draw the pedestrians' attention, I would switch the lights from low to high, and honk every once a while. I took extra precautions – I didn't want to run over anyone, and the streets were full of people. Some were shopping at small, kerosene lighted stands along the road, some were on their way back home from the fields, and others just went for a walk, talking to their friends, or heading to one of the local bars. I already got used to the fact that the locals consider the road built for pedestrians rather than cars.

Suddenly I could see a throng of people under the lights, entirely blocking the way. A fully loaded truck was stopped up the road. I pulled up. A few people immediately surrounded my car, knocking impatiently at the windows. At first glance, it was clear they wanted me to get out of the car. They seemed so excited that I – not knowing the reason – had no other option but to obey.

Right when I left the car, a few hands grabbed me, pushing me forward. The crowd parted, and I could see under the dim petroleum light the unmoving body of a man lying on the ground. I bent down to him. The man, around thirty, was still alive but the pain wouldn't let him move. "What happened?" I asked the curious fellows standing round. "He fell from up there," one man pointed to the truck standing nearby. "He got caught by a wire," the same man continued, pointing backwards. I followed his stretched arm, and saw, a few yards behind, a loosened electric cable at the height of about 15 feet. The truck driver simply didn't notice the loose electric cable, which swept his passenger away from the loaded deck. It was a very nasty fall.

"I will take him to the hospital," I decided, calling five young men and instructing them to gently lay the wounded man on the body of my car. "His spine must stay in the same position as now." I emphasized this, and watched them take action. Then I asked two of them to walk along the car, and keep the man company while protecting him from jolts.

"Where is the truck driver?" I asked the people before I got into my car. "The rat ran away, but he's being searched for. He'll get what he deserves." I hear spiteful cries coming from all sides.

"I remember it vividly," Joseph interrupts me, "some friends from the village gave him shelter. A good thing they did. Most probably, the aroused crowd would have killed him on the spot." Wait, Joseph," I argue, "he was innocent! That's out of the question!" In Africa whenever there is a car crash, the driver always bears the blame. The passenger, the pedestrian, the biker are ever at fault. The witnesses are more than happy to administer the justice themselves. "Listen to me," Joseph raises his forefinger, "if something of the sort happens to you, don't stop and drive straight away. How did the fellow do anyway?" Joseph asks curiously. "Oh, he had great luck. He didn't break a single bone; he only bruised his kidney. He stayed at the hospital for a few days and then he was allowed home. "So everything turned out well," Joseph laughs, "as far as I know, the truck driver also managed to escape." I keep my mouth shut. I am terribly happy that Joseph is behind the wheel.

We get to M'Bossembélé after three and a half hours of strenuous driving. We have only about 60 miles left to Bozoum. "We'll be home soon," Joseph announces. "Yes, with our car for sure," I am thinking while we are passing by one of Bossembélé small businesses. I can still recall vividly, a few weeks ago I had been standing there, wondering about how to get back to Bozoum.

I was then on my way from Bouar. The dentist Angelo was going south to the capital, and taking advantage of his trip, I rode with him a short ways. Angelo dropped me off at this very spot, and I had to continue in a different direction. It was a terrible furnace. The sun beat down so badly, I was determined to seek refuge from its burning beams under the shadow of the little shop. So I was sitting there, thinking of the local 'public transportation' I hadn't used until then, when I hear: "Bala-o, docteur," I turn around and see a young Arab greeting me. "What are you doing so far from your hospital?" he smiles. "Well, I'm just trying to get there," I say, holding back the surprise of being recognized even here. "So why don't you join me, my cab's coming back shortly." I see: the Arab is one of the local Bozoum marketers, who deliver goods from neighboring towns, and make extra money by transporting passengers. I happily accept his offer; I get to drive with someone who knows me, and this means a certain feeling of security. In good spirits, I get in the cab. It's an old Peugeot minivan, its body is all deformed and peeling. The car sits conspicuously low, which makes me a little concerned about the mufflers.

"You may take the VIP seat next to me," the driver opens the door. An Arabic rosary hangs on the rearview mirror, and the front is all covered with various promotional stickers. While I am shuffling in the front seat, the Arab and others are loading goods at the back of the truck: barrels with shortage oil and gas, various kinds of textiles, various instruments, and mainly a great number of sieves. "Is that for flour?" I ask. "Not at all, that's intended for sifting sand when seeking out diamonds. Since the time when some diamonds were found in Kunde, around the corner from Bozoum, this is a bestseller," the merchant relishes. Soon the whole body of the van is jammed with goods. Then they fix a few spare wheels onto the roof above our heads.

The Arab finally sits behind the wheel. Simultaneously, a guy about fifty, wearing a baseball hat and huge mirroring sunglasses pushes into the car. "Salaam," the driver greets him respectfully, and says to me quietly: "It's my boss." "Bonjour," I say to the boss, in French for a change. He just faintly nods his head, and without a single muscle moving in his face, pushes right next to me on the seat. I am squashed on the gearshift, and my previous notion of a comfortable journey vanishes. My good spirits forsake me. Soon other passengers walk up to the cab. They climb up the barrels and boxes, take their seats on the sides, on the luggage, the roof, and the attached tires, too. At the back and on the sides, their legs are hanging freely over the edges of the body, and soon, reminiscent of flies, they take hold of the entire car. When the fifteenth man takes his seat on the roof above me, I can't hold it any longer, and ask the Arab: "How many passengers do you take on board at most?" He just relocates his chewing gum to the other side of his mouth, and utters: "As many as can fit." Then he leans out of the window, shouting to the back: "Eh gweh? – Shall we go?" "Eh gweh! – Let's go!" Sounds from above in unison. We hit the road. We go slowly, there is no hurry, at 20 mph. The van squeaks, groans, wobbles, but we keep moving. About a mile behind the village, the engine hiccups a few times and fails. The Arab tries to restart the car a couple of times in vain. I had thought he would get out of the car and see what was wrong, but he is too much of a big gun for that. Two fifteen-year-old adolescents jump off of the roof, deftly open the hood, conjure a screwdriver and a set of wrenches, and quickly take out and clean the carburetor. They soon close the engine cover again, and jump back up on the roof. The driver starts the car again, and we slowly begin to move.

"Scoundrels," mutters the Arab. "Who?" I ask. "The gas sellers, of course," he says angrily. I think I know what he means. There is a true shortage of gas and diesel in the country; so the sellers, trying to make more money from the black market, mix the gasoline with petroleum and other additives. I keep eying the boss. His eyes are still hidden behind huge glasses, and he won't bat an eyelid. He remains stone-faced.

After a two-mile drive, the situation repeats. And then it repeats over and over again. I am desperate and cooked by the heat. Within an hour, we have covered less than 20 miles. Suddenly, I hear a rage of rapping on the roof. "What's happening?" I ask the Arab in surprise, as I see all the passengers jumping down from the body, running back up the road. Then I see them all vanish in the bush. "Don't ask me, I don't have a clue, "the driver says, getting out of the cabin. On the deck, there remained only a lame old man. "Where did everybody go?" I ask. "Oh, they caught sight of a crook, who owes them money. So they went to settle it straight away on the spot." explains the old man, without any concern. "Oh," is all I can say. It doesn't take long before my fellow passengers walk out of the bushes. With very content looks, they return to our vehicle. I don't care to ask about how they dealt with the crook. Soon everybody is sitting back on the roof, and we roll on.

The journey is pitiless, regularly interrupted by halts necessary for cleansing the carburetor. After three hours we finally make it to Bozoum. After the arrival, the driver collects money from the passengers. It's a standard procedure here: locals never pay in advance, one can't be sure the car will ever reach its destination. "How much do I owe you?" I ask the young Arab. "Nothing, of course. You're our doctor," for the first time I hear the boss' voice. I thank them both, and we all shake hands, but deep in my mind I know next time I will take a ride by a local cab only in a state of emergency.

While recalling the event I don't even notice we have covered a great deal of the journey. We are entering a dangerous road section with sharp turns. "I remember there used to be road signs here, with warnings about the sudden sharp turns," I say, wondering. "Didn't you hear about the diamond discovery in Kunde?" Joseph wonders, "people found the signs convenient, so they pulled them out, and created sieves out of them." "Yes, I did," I ensure Joseph, thinking of poor father Norbert, who shortly after the diamond discovery arrived at the Kunde village to check up on its school supported by the mission. He found nobody there. All the pupils and the professor had left for the nearby deposit. There haven't been any classes since then. "And do you know, there's actually a vast deposit of diamonds about 200 miles from Bozoum, adjoining the rainforest?" Joseph continues. "Yes, It's near Carnot. In February I went with some other people from the mission, just to take a look. I must say the diamond town really surprised me. It's so lively and rich! It reminded me of the American Wild West with its adventurers, and people craving for riches, and crooks and thieves, too."

"You're right," Joseph agrees. "Everyone who buys the license – strangers are the only exception – can start digging. And the natives – most of them hollow out just ordinary holes – and constantly search for their own treasure. "Joseph pauses for a moment, and then he adds: "There is an official ban for foreigners to buy the diamonds: they aren't even allowed to see them, actually. Unofficially, of course, it's all different."

I turn my attention back to the road. "The turns are really dangerous," I admire Joseph's adroitness. "Sure they are." Joseph agrees, "just a few years ago, this used to be the favorite resort of the ,saraginah' – the road bandits. Especially during the dry season the sparse bush grass allowed them to watch the arriving car from a distance. All they did was wait in the turn where the car

Any longer journey in Africa is always a small adventure.

had to slow down, and give it a burst from the automatic. Fortunately, it's quiet here now. Still, the Arabian merchants hire soldiers to accompany their columns of trucks. For three years already, nobody has spotted saraginah here. They work now more in the northern and eastern part of the country."

Joseph is right. The last case I remember occurred about 6 months ago, about 300 miles east from here near the city of Bambari. The local priest and a nun were on their way from Bangui. The road bandits descended on them. The priest determined not to stop and drive away. That was a fatal mistake. Had he stopped, the bandits might have only robbed them, but now they open fire. One bullet killed the nun, another bullet injured the priest, but he managed to arrive at Bambari despite the wound. This evoked anger in the local people, who set up a funeral procession with ten cars, carrying the body of the dead nun to Bangui. But at the same spot as before the cortege was attacked by the same bandits, who entirely ransacked it. People talked a lot about it; there was even a protest demonstration in the capital city. The government, however, hasn't started dealing with the problem of bandits yet. Who cares in the capital city about things so many miles away!

Eventually, the familiar hills rise on the horizon. This time we arrive safely. Even Joseph looks content; any longer journey in Africa is always a small adventure.

Chapter Sixteen

Every Country Has Its Customs

One day Gerome's wife came to our maternity ward. She gave birth to a pretty little girl. When I was driving from the hospital back to the mission in the afternoon, I ran into our cook on his way in from the field. I slow down and call out from the window: "Gerome, you have a daughter, would you like to take a look at her? I will drive you to the hospital." "Yes, I'll be glad," Gerome agrees, taking a seat next to mine. Soon we are entering the room where his wife is resting. "Look," I remove the tip of the cloth wrapping the newborn. A faint smile appears on Gerome's face. "I better leave you alone now," I say, attempting to sneak away from the room. "Wait," Gerome runs down to me, "you want to leave me here?" I am at a loss. "I thought you wanted to stay a while with your wife and the baby, am I right?" I say in surprise. "Well, I did see the baby, and there ain't much to do here any longer," Gerome shakes his head, and rushes to the car. I don't know what to say. Suddenly I recall the halls of our European maternity wards, jammed with congratulating husbands and relatives, who can't wait to see the baby. Mother's tables, full of flowers and delicacies. It was later I found out that Gerome is not a monster, that he really loves his wife and his children; he merely doesn't put it on display. It's not a custom in Africa. To put it

One day Gerome's wife came to our maternity ward. She gave birth to a pretty little girl.

bluntly, every country has its customs. You won't ever see a boy holding his girlfriend's hand, let alone giving her a kiss in public. During my stay I also attended a few weddings. I had thought that at least on this occasion, the groom is to give the bride a wedding kiss. I was mistaken; it isn't a custom here. It isn't appropriate to put one's feelings on display.

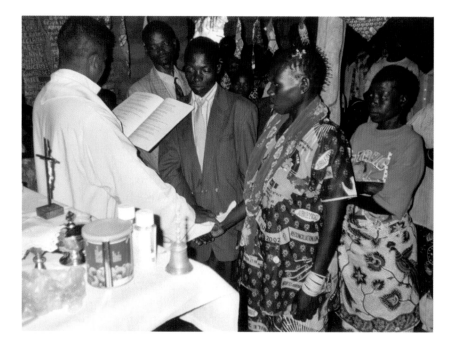

During my African stay I also attended a few weddings. (Page131)

The only exception is the death of a close relative. The local customs virtually ask for it. In the hospital, I have often been confronted with moaners, who would lament and wring their hands. In grief they would fall to the ground and throw dust into the air. Traditions associated with grieving make a very distinct part of the local habits. During these occasions, the mourners make a gathering "place mortuaire" in the house of the deceased, bemoaning the dead and bidding farewell. If a man dies, the funeral ceremony lasts for three nights, if a woman dies, it lasts one night more. The first day before the funeral, the body is laid under the shelter of his house, and then mainly just the relatives stay with the dead in silence and meditation. They sing and pray. A funeral follows, the dead is laid to rest. The evenings after funerals are sort of like great family gatherings. It's a unique occasion when all members of the extended families join together. There are fires in front of the house of the dead burning all night, there are drums and singing and, of course, a funeral feast when the members of the family cast their minds back on the one who had left.

Every time I saw the natives dancing at the funeral ceremony, it seemed really strange. In Europe, the dance concerns mainly a couple, the man and the woman, and comes with merry occasions and celebrations. In Africa, however, its significance is much deeper. "Dance, that's our life," says my colleague Albert. "You can dance in a group, when there's two of you, or alone. There's always an opportunity to dance. Through dance you can express everything – joy, love, sadness, despair. Watch sometimes the old African women dancing at a child's funeral. You will understand for sure what their dancing means." He was right. The dance was very much different from the village festivities. No one has to push the Africans to dance. It's a part of their everyday life.

I recall the Easter I spent in a small village forlorn in the bush, about 25 miles from Bozoum. I gave company to father Sebastian who was there to celebrate an open-air Holy Saturday Mass. He needed someone to be in charge of the lighting. We brought from Bozoum a small dynamo powered by a gasoline engine and a few bulbs. I climbed a few trees to hang the bulbs up there and then I wired them together. After sunset, I turned on the dynamo. For the villagers, this was a true miracle. The village flared with a light they hadn't known before. From the very beginning I could sense the villagers were filled with great joy. Joy that their priest came to them – the distant location makes them see him only every few weeks – and they were happy from the "shining lights". It was during the mass that the rows of people started to slowly sway in rhythm, and then they began to clap for joy and swing, and the service then smoothly traversed to a spontaneous village celebration. The natives wouldn't go home after the end of the mass. They took us among themselves,

It is not rare to witness even five-year-old girls importantly carrying their one-year-old cousins tied onto their back.

brought the drums, and we danced! No one minded the bulbs going off a good while ago, and that the village fires hadn't been lighted yet. Dozens of villagers started dancing in riveting rhythm with the drums, and I could hardly discern the stamping feet of villagers wildly whirling the dust that was densely rising up to the night sky. I see their flashing black curly heads and rejoicing arms flickering against the paler sky. The only thing I could see through the night and the clouds of dust more clearly, was the white of their glittering eyes. It was an unforgettable experience for me. Easter was really full of pleasure and joy.

Family is the fundamental feature, and the key to understanding the African community. In Africa, it isn't only father, mother and children like back home in most cases, but a richly diversified community with grandparents, uncles, and aunts with their children. The average African woman has eight children, such a community then often includes dozens of members who live in houses standing right next to one another, constituting a substantial part of the village or city neighborhood. In principle, mothers usually take care only of their smallest which they breastfeed. When the kids grow up a little all the relatives care for them, the whole family pitches in. Elder sisters or cousins often take up the mother's role. It's not rare to witness five-year-old girls importantly carrying one-year-old cousins tied onto their back.

This substitution of roles reflects itself also in the ambiguity of certain words. The expression "Mama tih mbih – My mother" refers to both mother and aunt. Also, the expression "ita" refers to brother, sister, and cousin. This might lead to confusion for ones who aren't familiar with it. There was a nurse in our hospital, and I knew he had a few brothers, but just two sisters. When he brought up to me the fifth woman asking me to examine his sister "out of acquaintance", I couldn't stand it any longer, and asked him to stop making fun of me. He wasn't making fun of me. The notions "sister" and "female cousin" coincide in Africa.

Chapter Seventeen

Iron

A young girl unlashes a large, colorful bandanna from behind her back. She brought a tiny suckling baby in it. She places him on the bed, and gives me a questioning look. The child lies helplessly, like a broken toy, his eyes are closed and he breathes rapidly. I notice his little hands with palms white as snow contrasting loudly with his black skin. I carefully flip over the bottom eyelid – and again the sinister white. I touch his forehead – fever. I gently slide my hand to the little body and feel the heart beating hastily. With my other hand I touch the stomach. Both the spleen and the liver are huge. "Semplice," I call the head nurse from the pediatrics ward, "the child must get a blood transfusion, and start malaria treatment immediately." "I'm sorry, but we ran out of transfusion sachets," Semplice shrugs his shoulders. "There are still a few left in a box at the mission," I remember. It was sent as a gift from some Swiss woman a few months ago. "And there's only a few remaining HIV tests," Semplice adds with the same tone. There is no blood bank in Bozoum. When a transfusion is needed, one must search for a donor among the relatives, and the donor should test HIV Negative, of course. But these tests are difficult to obtain in Bozoum, and I have none left at the mission. "Try the mother, first of all," I decide, "and if she is of the right blood group, don't do the HIV test, just give him the blood straight away." I have no time to lose. "I'll bring the sachet," I call back at Semplice, as I run to the car. Soon I return. Semplice impatiently grabs the sachet, and rushes to the ill child. I go to the operation hall, where I execute a scheduled hernia operation.

In less then an hour I hear knocking. "Yes," I say, looking carefully from behind the screen. Semplice pushes his head in the half-opened door, and looks at me unhappily: "A kwih, mon docteur – The baby died, doctor." I just cast my eyes down to the wound, and say nothing. It's the sixth child this week. Again, the parents came too late to the hospital. It was a badly neglected case of chronic malaria. Without any doubt, the child's death resulted from severe anemia, not the infection itself. I can fully understand Semplice's feelings. It happened to me here, too, a child died in front of my eyes right before I could set up the transfusion.

"Albert," I turn to my assistant after some silence, "this is impossible. I've been working here for a number of months, but there've never been so many child deaths." Albert isn't surprised: "Don't forget, doctor, that the rainy season has just ended, and that's the time when mosquitoes – the carriers of malaria – are swarming. Moreover, it's the time of harvest. Parents must work all day long in the fields, to have something to eat in the following months. They can't spend a week at the hospital with their child, and that's why they come when it's too late already. When it's too late," he repeats and adds: "That's how it goes, year after year."

We spend the evening on the veranda, watching the red lights of the fireplaces in front of the huts. I keep thinking of the dead children. There must be someway out of this, but what? I don't know. Suddenly, I hear coughing behind me. I turn around and see Alfonso, the night watchman of the mission. "Mwenih kolih ah gah ti bah moh – Some people are looking for you," he announces. I stand up and walk to the gate. Frightened eyes gaze at me at the gate: "Mwenih molengeh... Moh gah nah hospital... – A child, quickly...go to the hospital..." I don't understand much from the waterfall of their shouting utterances, but I get it. They are the relatives of a patient, and were sent by a nurse to bring me. I quickly get into a car. Alfonso comes up, and readily opens the gate. Once at the hospital, I head straight away to the pediatrics ward. The relatives bring me to a bed; Semplice is there, too. I illuminate the bed by flashlight. A slender foot of the toddler sticks out of the rags. The sole is white as snow, again. I unwrap the baby. It's a sinister case, just like in the morning. "Yes," I turn to Semplice, "let me give you a sachet for transfusion." "Thanks," Semplice nods his head, "but we have another problem. Much worse." "What?" I ask, recalling unwittingly Anastasio's words: nothing ever goes smoothly in Africa. "We can't detect the blood group, the lab technician isn't at home. He went downtown, and nobody of the family knows where he put the keys to the lab. We just can't get hold of him." This is really a problem. Without the relevant reagents I can't find out the baby's blood group, or the donor's for that matter. And time flies. I hear the little boy breathing quickly in the dark. Without the transfusion he is going to die this very night.

An idea sparkles in my head. "Turn on the generator, so there's light," I say, "I'll be right back," I call Semplice, running out into the night. I drive as quickly as I can back to the mission. I turn to the sister's house straight away. I remembered the missionaries telling me that sister Christiane, when she was still in charge of the pediatrics ward, repeatedly donated blood to her patients. She is type "O", the universal donor, and our only hope.

"Christiane," I speak to the elderly sister, "A one-year-old baby is dying at the hospital…"

I knock at the door, and quietly walk inside. The sisters sit around the table, having dinner. "Christiane," I speak to the elderly sister, "A one-year-old baby is dying at the hospital and needs blood badly. A knife clinks in the silence. Christiane stands, and hurriedly follows me to the car. When we walk down the stairs I realize she is like a wisp. She can't weigh more than 90 pounds. I am sorry to ask her for this, but I have no other option.

When we approach the hospital, the windows of the pediatrics ward are shining. Christiane slides calmly after me into the room of the sick baby, and looks around in concern. Her eyes come alive. A smile appears on her wrinkled face. Memories. She had spent thirty long years here. "Christiane, Christiane…" I hear the natives whisper from all sides. They reach their hands, and greet her with joy. Taking short, vital steps she walks across the room to the sick child, hastily clasping the patients' hands. Semplice, still waiting by the little patient, respectfully greets her: "Bonsoir ma soeur." I feel, that although Christiane hasn't worked here for some time already, she is still the lady of the house. She glances at the child, without examining it; she throws her hands up, and hastily rolls up her sleeve. "Vite, vite – quickly, quickly," she whispers, reaching her slender arm to me.

Soon the blood is dripping into the little boy's vein, and I drive Christiane back to the mission. "Thank you," I gratefully look at her. "It was nothing, I am glad you came to me," she waves her hand.

"It turned out well, then," I happily say to myself, "but this is no permanent solution." When a baby in such condition comes tomorrow, I cannot ask her for blood again, she doesn't have that much herself! The best solution would be if the mothers came to the hospital sooner, so the treatment could proceed without transfusion.

The next day is Sunday. I wake up a little sooner. I hear the irregular putt-putt of a car: father Marcello is trying to start up his automobile. Every Sunday early in the morning he sets out to celebrate mass at a church at the other side of town. When he returns another mass awaits him here at the mission. I have an idea. I hastily put my clothes on, and run outside. "Wait for me, I will go with you," I shout at Marcello, and jump in the starting car. On the way, I share with him the plan. He nods in agreement: "Try it, you'll see." At the end of the mass, Marcello holds up the attendees: "Just one minute before you go, doctor Marcel has something to tell you." I walk up, and face the natives. I hold a scrap of paper in my hand, from which I read my improvised speech: "Aitah tih mbih… Dear friends! Many people died at the hospital recently. This is not good. If you have children at home who are always tired, don't play, have white palms, please bring them to the hospital today in the afternoon or tomorrow. If you see such children at your neighbors', bring them, too. I will prescribe them medicine. If you don't have money for the medicine, you can have it for free."

The Bozoumers, who have been quietly listening until now, clasp their hands and scream in enthusiasm. Something is going to be for free! This is hot news to tell. And that was my plan. There is no radio station, or newspaper in the city, but this news will definitely spread from hut to hut. Before lunch, I attend the second mass with Marcelo, and I repeat what I said. Then I just wait for whatever will happen.

In fact, the first mothers start to gather at the mission gate in the afternoon. They carry their offspring in bundles on their back, or in their arms, or hold them by the hand. The frightened cries of the children reverberate.

I fetch a box of Nivaquin against Malaria, and another with Iron pills from the mission storehouse. There's already a throng of people standing at the gate. "One after another," I say, taking the first child in my arms. It struggles against me and cries desperately. "Good, it seems just strong enough," I say to myself, examining its palms and conjunctivas. It doesn't suffer from anemia, only its tiny nose is all smudged. He has a runny nose, that's all. "Nzonih – Good," I say to the mother, giving her the child back. The next kid is doing fine, too, it's only some intestinal parasite disease. The third child, however, is very pale, and looks at me sadly and wearily. "I must do something with this child, or they will bring it to me in a few days dying," I say to myself. "Mama, moh kuh mbih – Wait a moment there, mother," I ask the woman to take a seat at the nearby wall. "Next!" I shout to the crowd. The forth child has malaria, but it isn't anemic. I hand Nivaquin to the mother and turn to a new patient. In the meantime, the first two mothers – with already examined children – press on to the front. Violently they push away others, scream, pull at my clothes, angrily gesticulate and keep shoving their – generally speaking – healthy offspring. With a grudge they point to the child sick with malaria, who got the medicine. Other women run out of the line, agitated, joining the two, and start to quarrel. There's terrible chaos. I swiftly take my cans with medicine, and run away, searching for refuge at a nearby small house, at the corner of the mission grounds. Marcelo occasionally teaches catechism there. Fortunately it's empty now. In the last moment I manage to slam the door shut as the aroused crowd of women just reach it. What am I to do now? I hear the bustle and bangs hit the door. I peep out like a prisoner from a barred window. There are a few teenagers chasing a ball on the dusty yard in front of the mission. "Alah gah geh – Come here!" I call them in desperation. "Help me, and when it's over, you'll get a keteh kadoh – a small present." They respond quickly. They come, and vehemently push their way to the door through the throng.

Briefly, I initiate them in the plan. The room where I have found refuge has two doors. I need them to allow a couple of mothers at a time to go inside with their children, and as soon as I examine them, let them out through the other door. And then let the next mothers in again. That was the deal, and then we could start.

The two notorious mothers push through the door first, of course. They still keep shouting and wildly throw apart their hands. I reach into my can, fishing out pills of Iron for their healthy children. I give five pieces to each of them. So both mothers have obtained, at least, some kind of "yoro – medicine" for their babies. They smile happily, and contentedly leave the room. I am aware the pills can do no harm; moreover, about 80% of the local population suffers from a certain level of Iron deficiency. I can't reflect upon this any longer, because here comes another group. The kids with malaria without anemia get Nivaquin, the very pale ones I ask to wait at the mission wall, and all others get a few pills of Iron, because all the mothers categorically demand free "yoro" for their children. This goes on until the evening. Among a hundred babies I find three that need immediate hospitalization. After the end of the action, I reward the willing boys with a few small coins, and I quickly head to the mothers, who are still waiting for me in front of the mission. "Fadesoh eh gweh nah pediatrie – We shall now go to the pediatrics ward," and I ask them to get into my Citroën. The children are seriously sick, but if we launch the treatment today, they still have a good chance for recovery. A few days later would be too late.

Introduction

It was in the winter of 1998 that I first met Marcel Drlík, a 28-years-old doctor, pursuing his career in the third year of vascular surgery of Charles University in Prague. He was willing to work in his field as a volunteer in Africa. He would ask and I would smile, replying that African medical centers won't really meet his expectations. I offered him work in the Bozoum Hospital, the parish of our mission in Central African Republic. In January 2000, after 6-month course of Tropical Medicine in Lyon, he set out for his adventure.

From February, letters would arrive to Prague, addressed to Marcel's grandmother. I read them, too, and eagerly, and made xerox copies, which I would later hand out to visitors of our church of the Virgin Mary Victorious. Christian love to the poor was radiating from the lines. (During the Communist Era, the author was the only one from his class going to Church; it was tolerated because he was the best pupil.) Then it crossed my mind to publish these letters. When I asked him in Bozoum the following March, he wasn't really thrilled about it. He said he never really wrote. I didn't give up and kept telling him he could always start. His challenging work shifts did not help much, however, and time flew. The coup d'état of October 25, 2002, and following guerilla warfare which ended finally in March 2003 by the victory of the new president François Bozizé, came quite without attention of Czech people. Marcel decided to change this, started working and soon, in October 2003, his book appeared in Prague bookstores and virtually became a bestseller.

Dr. Marcel Drlík – influenced by his Bozoum experience – changed his field to pediatrics and has visited the mission many times since, and is now trying to establish partnership between the Charles University in Prague and the University in Bangui.

O. Anastasio Roggero, OCD

Carmelite Mission
in Central African Republic

The next day, I set out all weary to the hospital. The African weekends are never long. It's not a time to rest.

Driving down the hill, I come across unusual multitudes of people. They are mostly women carrying their bundles. "What's going on here?" I wonder. "Is some unique market downtown today?" When I reach the hospital, I begin to understand. I guess this won't make the hospital staff very happy. From the distance I see the throngs besieging the pediatrics ward. Semplice stands on the veranda, desperately wringing his hands, calling me: "Doctor, come here, all these women ask me for some medicine. They say you promised it to them. For free. You know, nothing is free in the hospital." He is right. This is a state hospital, and for the past two years the State has neither paid its employees, nor invested in the maintenance of hospital equipment. The only chance to obtain the means to run the hospital is by the sale of medicine; it is purchased at the capital and sold here with a small surcharge.

"Here, take this." I hand him my cans with Iron and Nivaquin, asking him to examine the children carefully, and possibly, to hospitalize the anemic children. Now Semplice understands. He smiles. He sees already what this unbelievable chaos is about. He calls some other nurses, and everyone gets down to work. Some examine the children, some write down the names of the comers – so they wouldn't come repeatedly for medicine, and some reward the healthy children with a few pills of Iron. Before noon, we managed to examine about a hundred and fifty children. Again, we found among them some severely anemic children. The next day, the situation was similar. The only difference was that now there was about three hundred. The hospital was bursting with running, shouting, playing and crying kids. Their mothers cruised among them in colorful clothes, some wore bandanas on their heads, others parasols. They filled the waiting time with a loud chatter. The Bozoum marketplace grew into a calm and quiet spot these days.

"Ah Unzi aweh – We ran out!" Desperately Semplice runs to me, and turns the can upside down to show me there is no Iron

The most important thing was that no more children would die of anemia in the following weeks.

anymore. "Every mother wants medicine for her child," he heatedly explains. I try to calm him down. "Is there some Iron still at the pharmacy?" "Yes," Semplice replies, about two cans. "Here is some money, and you can proceed," I put some banknotes in his hand. He bursts out happily with relief: "Thanks, doctor, I was just picturing myself being lynched by all these enraged women."

The repeated "mob raids" on the hospital went on in the next days, until the end of the week. I guess the nurses had the unique chance to examine the health of the vast majority of Bozoum children. Mothers just brought into the hospital all their children, both healthy, and sick. I gradually ran out of medicine and money. After consulting the hospital accountant, my colleague finally managed to get the rest of the Iron in store for free, so that no mother would leave the hospital empty-handed.

By the end of the week, there was not a single pill of Iron in the hospital; the pediatrics ward, however, was full of anemic children. We would get new Iron as soon as someone goes to Bangui. The most important thing was that no more children would die of anemia in the following weeks.

Chapter Eighteen

Going to the Rainforest

I watch the mosquitoes and night butterflies orbiting the lamp
at the veranda in a wild whirl. I lean over the armrest of my chair,
waiting with the others for Sebastian, who hasn't arrived yet. Here
he finally comes. Father Marcello says a short prayer, blesses the
food, and we all sit down around the table. Dinner is usually the
only chance for me to see all the people in the mission. These are
the moments when we all can talk together, share what happened
during the day, or make plans, and it's fun.

I look over the table at Jan. We are the only two Czechs in the
Central African Republic. Since August he has been working as a
volunteer in the local kindergarten, after Francesca who had
returned back to Italy in the summer. Before he came to Bozoum

146

he had worked in the Czech Republic with Romany children, so he has experience. I am happy he is here. I can finally talk to someone in Czech and Jan is a very pleasant and easy-going person.

I watch him as he fishes some sort of drowning insect out of his soup. He places it at the rim of the plate, and then goes on eating, as if nothing happened. "Listen, Jan, when I came to Bozoum, sister Marina informed me that there were three levels of adaptation to Africa: One, a fly gets into your soup and you pour the soup out. Two, you take it out and you carry on eating. Three, you leave it in your bowl and you eat the fly. I am glad you're getting used to things." "Well, if that is the case, then our Norberto has reached level four. He will eat anything, absolutely anything." Marcelo pokes fun at his neighbor. We all laugh; Norberto's appetite is phenomenal.

"I guess you all know that in four days two Czech journalists are coming to shoot a documentary for Czech Television about the Central African Republic, and our mission here." "New Czechs! The highest number of Czechs in the history of the country!" I say to myself, and Marcello continues: "We must pick them up in Bangui, and bring them here. They will carry on to Bouar from here. Our doctor's going to show them around, he speaks Czech, French and Sango. And throughout the year he has learned something about Africa as well, haven't you?" and he gives me a friendly wink. I was aware of this before, so I nod. "Marcel, you are to go by yourself," he says, "I can't do without the others here." "But what if something goes wrong with the car? It's more than 600 miles roundtrip," I object, "I can change a wheel, but that's all." "Well, I can ask our mechanic Joseph to join you, so you won't worry." "Can I go, too?" Jan asks vehemently. "I'd love to take a closer look at the capital." "Why not," Marcello smiles, "ask the doctor then."

We set out to Bangui in three days, the three of us, Joseph, Jan, and I. I drive in the beginning, but then I am happy to pass the wheel to Joseph. He is much more experienced, and drives faster and safer. My compatriot watches the surrounding bush with keen interest. "How long does it take from Bangui to the rainforest?" he suddenly asks Joseph. "It's just about 10 miles west, towards M'Baiki. The rainforest starts there," the driver replies keeping his eyes glued to the road, which is now in poor condition after the rainy season. Every minute he has to evade potholes. "Well, we could take a look over there, couldn't we?" Jan reflects. "No, we can't," I ruin his hopes, "we reach Bangui in the afternoon, spend the night in the Centre d'accueil, and as soon as we pick up the journalists at the airport, we have to return." "It's a pity," Jan grumbles. "And you've been to the rainforest?" "Yes, once," I nod. "How was it?" Jan asks. I don't really hear him.

Looking out of the car, my mind drifts four months back in time. Behind the window, there is no grass, and bush, but merely a continuous green rampart of tall, huge trees. I am picturing our pygmy guide, jumping out of the body of our van, and skillfully pushing his way through the thick shrubbery. The bushes reach up to his shoulders. Soon he lifts a flimsy wooden bar, which marks the entrance to the Dzanga-Sanga National Park. He waves at us to go. Very slowly we drive through. The rainforest reaches its long limbs at us; the branches then close behind like a curtain. "Welcome to Jurassic Park," utters Aurelio behind the wheel, and he adds, "Let's wait for the guide to get back, and then we shall carry on. "

It's been raining recently. The road is full of slimy red mud and puddles. We drive at a walking pace. The wheels keep slipping and it rains at us heartily from the trees. Every minute we bog down into the mud, and have to re-start our four-wheel-drive jeep. Despite these hardships we slowly move on. After an hour-long exhausting drive, our guide bangs on the roof, giving us a signal that the car won't go any further. We have to continue on foot.

Tropical rainforest revels with all colors.

I get out of the car, and I sink right away into the damp, mushy earth. All around it's dim. The three branches above us create a majestic arch of a sort of huge gothic cathedral; raindrops keep falling on our heads from the branches. The rainy season lasts in the rainforest all year round. We can call ourselves lucky concerning the weather, though. For the time being it's not raining. Curiously I look around. We stand on a clearing; the path forms a wide loop and turns back again. There are huge trees towering, with lianas growing over them. I used to think until now that the tropical rainforest revels with all the colors of fabulous wild orchids, but it's not like that. In vain I search for a color different than green. But it fascinates me by all its shades – on a scale between bright green, the color of our sprouting grass, and dark, dim green reminiscent of our pine forests. I inhale deeply. I smell the light scent of moldering leaves mixed with other unknown fragrances, distantly reminding me of a fruit orchard. The rainforest stretches hundreds of miles in all directions.

We got here from the Bozoum plateau, traveling almost 400 miles on bad, clay roads. We kept heading south, down the hill. Never before had I undergone such a long descent. I felt we were going to the core of the earth. I still wonder. This is then what the end of the world looks like. From here, one can continue only on foot, or on piragua up the Sangha River.

The place were the Central African Republic meets Congo and Cameroon: the Congo Basin rimmed by the Sangha, Lobaye and Oubangui Rivers, is considered by some naturalists the best preserved rainforest on the Earth, and at the same time a blind spot on the map, very little explored until now. The Dzangha-Sangha National Park, where we are now, stretches over the northern part of the area. However, this isn't a safari welcoming thousands of tourists, because tourists don't visit the Central African Republic and no tourists would ever travel to the far-flung national park. Perhaps it's a pity, since there are animals one can hardly see elsewhere: the rainforest elephant, the bongo antelope, the lowland gorilla, etc. In the legends of the Aka tribe of Pygmies there is mention of a certain huge animal, a prehistoric monster still remaining unseen. The natives call it "Mokele". They say it resembles a cross between a unicorn and a dinosaur. The huge herbivore can easily kill an elephant.

"Ala mah mbi – Listen," I recall again the five-foot tall, sinewy Pygmy tracker who happens to be our guide. His large, dark eyes loom up from under chiseled ridges with huge dense eyebrows. He wears a light shirt, short pants, and a machete over his shoulder. Although he doesn't speak French, the management of the national park is happy to employ him; just like all Pygmies, he is simply at home in the rainforest. I remember vividly when he approached our group and with a big smile he instructed us in

All Pygmies feel in the rainforest at home.

Sango: "If you want the trip to turn out well, you must be silent from now on. The rainforest is so thick that an elephant can stand 10 feet from you, and you won't see it. That's why I must hear what's happening around. Watch carefully for the snakes above your head, and also watch your feet not to cross the way of black ants. If you meet a gorilla, stop, squat down, don't move, and primarily, avoid eye contact. It's going to leave you alone then. If we bump into an elephant, do the same as me." He took a short pause, and then he continued: "Now we're going to walk a few miles on animal routes up to a clearing with salt springs, called "Bai" in our native tongue. On its side, there stands a small, wooden observation post that's going to protect us from the animals. But the way to get there is always a risk. All around, there are many animals coming to lick salt. One must take precautions. And now, if you're ready, let's go," the tracker ends his speech.

I take a look at the others. There stands Francesca, a teacher from Bozoum; my old acquaintance Angelo, a dentist, who joined us from Bouar; Stephania, a teacher in Yolé lyceum; and father Aurelio, who came from Yolé also. Everyone except me is Italian. We had planned the trip for several weeks, and we share its costs.

The tracker swiftly hits the trail. He walks first. He cuts our way with his machete, and we follow him closely. Although he is the smallest of us, we are having a hard time keeping pace with him. Soon the trail leads us to the bank of a small stream. "We're going to walk through water, there's no other way." I take my shoes off. The water is pleasantly warm, and the streambed is soft. I walk comfortably barefoot, and I must admit our guide did a good job in planning the journey. It's far easier to walk here than on the thin route full of branches and roots. I notice round pools filled with water on the banks. "Andoli – Elephants," the Pygmy remarks, pointing to the huge tracks. There is also heaps of elephant dung on the way. Some of it is still warm. The animals can't be far away. After a hundred-yard walk on the riverbed, we climb back on bank, and struggle through the rainforest again. Suddenly the guide stops. He gives us a sharp wave to stop. Attentively he listens to a remote cracking noise. After a while he carelessly sweeps his hand, and says: "Macaque." Within a minute, a monkey jumps the branches high above our heads. I find myself in admiration of the native's ability to tell the animal just from the very sound.

Finally, we get to the edge of the clearing. When we climb up the raised stand, about 20 feet high, there opens up a fabulous view. We sit stunned. In the clearing of about a 1/3-mile in diameter, walled off by a rampart of giant trees, there is a system of salt pools, connected with small streams. About twenty elephants, young and adult, are bathing and licking salt. At a

About twenty elephants, young and adult, are bathing and licking salt.

respectful distance from them buffalo are lying, and antelopes are taking a stroll. Suddenly, a flock of a few hundred colorful parrots fly above our heads. I watch the performance in fascination. Nowhere in the world can the rainforest animals be observed as easily as here. Although the random observations of travelers had given evidence of elephants in the rainforest, up until the first half of the twentieth century it was considered a strange species of small, "pygmy" elephant. It was later – and with the discovery of these salt pools, which offer the best possible spot for observation, that this error was clarified. It's not a new species, but the same species of African elephant known from the savannahs – only its behavior is different. In the savannahs, elephants stay in herds, protecting their young from lions. Here in the rainforest, elephants have no natural enemy, so one can often spot young elephants wandering alone. And from these random encounters sprang up legends about the small, "pygmy" elephant.

The loud trumpeting and bubbling of trunks under water resounds across the clearing. While some elephants are coming, others vanish in the thickness of the tropical rainforest. We all eagerly take pictures and lose track of the time going by. We don't even notice that the sky grows dark, and dusk comes to the forest. But now the Pygmy hints it's high time to head back. Suddenly, the first raindrops fall on our heads. The light rain soon changes to a hard, tropical downpour. The earth at once turns to mud. I have only one pair of shoes on me, and since I don't want to obliterate them entirely, I walk barefoot like our guide. I am all sopping, soaking wet and muddy from head to foot. It's very hard to stay clean in the rainforest.

"Marcel, we could still give it a try," Jan interrupts me and I lose my train of thought. The desire to see the rainforest just gives him no rest. "We'll see, ok?" I concede, "I'd also like to see the forest once more in my life."

We arrive in Bangui in the afternoon only to hear the plane won't arrive in the morning. They tell us there isn't enough avgas at the airport, and the plane couldn't return back to Paris. No wonder the French pilots don't feel like going under such circumstances. The only thing we can do is wait. Luckily, the next day we hear the good news: "The plane will arrive after midnight."

This gives us a whole day. "Marcel, the forest..." Jan reminds me again. "Well, why not actually, we could give it a try," I concede, thinking I heard or read somewhere that southwest of the capital, in the rainforest on the bank of Oubangui, there is a port. "There must be some way of going there!" I confide to

154

Joseph, trying to see, if he could take us there. "You're the boss here, doctor," he says, "I'll be happy to go with you, I just want to say, that I am a Central African, and I have never heard of this port of yours." "It doesn't matter," I calm him, "we just want to see at least something from the forest. Let's just drive in that direction, and if there is no way to go any further, we will return."

We set out right from the airport. Joseph asks for the way to the port at a military station at the edge of town. Soon he returns bringing good news: "Yes, the port exists," he tells us with enthusiasm, "in about 3 miles there is a turn south the lumberjacks use. We can't miss it – it's the only one. Then it's about 60 miles." "That's great," I rejoice, "we can just drive for a little bit through the forest, we don't have to go all the way to the river." Determined, I say to Joseph. "Let's go!"

The clay road we start on is quite decent. Jan gets carried away. We both admire the stunning beauty of the virgin forest, the gigantic trees with roots high above the ground. Every once in a while we drive by little villages, surrounded by the necessary small fields, on which the natives grow manioc and corn. After about 20 miles, the surface of the road rapidly changes. It's really bad. The road is all furrowed up by tractors, which the lumberjacks use for transporting the fallen trees. It's full of potholes, with water to the top. After an hour drive, we have to stop the car. The road disappears in water. For a good hundred yards, the rainforest is all flooded, and only long poles reaching out of the water show the way. We step out of the car and look around. "I guess we'll have to return," I say to Joseph, "we can't drive through this." I think I hurt his professional driver's pride, because he grins and says with self-confidence: "You say we won't? Well, get in, and we shall see!" And he starts up the Mitsubishi again. "The key to success is keeping a slow pace and never stop." Just as he finishes the sentence, the car jerks forward, and we get stuck in the swamp for good. "Well, good job!" I grin, "we're stuck cabin-deep in a swamp, and the nearest habitation is 30 miles from here.

On the other side we can see a rusty, iron riverboat that could transport trucks even.

Moreover, by the evening we have to be at the airport, to pick up the journalists. How stupid of me to drive with you to the rainforest, just for fun!" "Just relax, doctor," Joseph says, keeping a stiff upper lip, and cautiously opens the door of the car. The water reaches right below the floor. Joseph climbs up to the roof, and crawling over the front glass, he reaches over the engine hood. He leans his head down, and turns on the four-wheel drive. Then he climbs back to the cabin, slowly and intermittently he steps on the gas. And so, engaging all four wheels, he rocks the imprisoned car. After a while, he manages to get out of the unlucky spot, and we proceed! Off we go; Joseph really made it.

"Bravo!" Jan and I applaud. The driver is happy. I just don't know how our trip back will turn out.

Another hour goes by, and coming across no single human dwelling, we reach the wide river. There isn't any bridge. On the other side we can see a rusty, iron riverboat that could transport trucks even. There are a few people standing by it. We wave and shout. Soon, a pirogue with a few workers leaps off. "If you want to get across to the other side, you must lend us your accumulator," the boss explains, stepping out of the boat, "ours is entirely discharged." Joseph opens the hood without hesitation and takes the battery out. "I guess that's how it works here," I catch my breath. "If those guys don't speak the truth, and disappear with our battery on the other side, we're lost for good," I remark, watching the natives crossing the river back.

It turns out Joseph's estimate was better than mine. Soon we hear the roar of a starting diesel engine and we watch the iron ship approaching our bank. We pay the transport fee, and get our battery back. "This is a border region, you need to enter your names into the logbook," the captain approaches me, assuming I am the boss, because I sat next to the driver. I don't have a clue where we are, but I give him a nod. The captain glimpses at the inscription on our car door "Mission Catholique", starting a conversation. "You must be going to the Mogumba Mission, am I right?" he inquires. I smile. Unwittingly, the man gave me precious information. I fill out the column "From: Bangui – To: Mission de Mogumba" without any hesitation. "How far are we?" I ask the sailor. "It's less then 6 miles, you're almost there," he replies, waving goodbye.

Yes, soon we reach a small town. "Are you hungry? They said there was a mission down here." "Let's go there," Jan reads my thoughts. We ask for the way at a marketplace nearby. Soon, we pull up by a small church with two bells. A small house with a garden stands next to it. "Let me find out, whether the mission is inhabited," I suggest to the others, slowly extricating ourselves from the car. I walk to the house, then at once the door opens, and two girls are standing there. The younger smiles, and keenly welcomes me: "Hey Marcel, so you managed to visit us in the end! Don't stand outside and please come in!" she summons my friends. "You've made it just for lunch." I am completely perplexed. We've been driving 80 miles at random through the rainforest to arrive at our acquaintances' for lunch. I am trying to conceal my surprise. I pretend we really came for a scheduled visit. But – at the same time – I am trying to figure out how come the girl happens to know me. We start a conversation, and I carefully try to find out. It comes out that eight months ago she attended in Bangui the meeting of ASSOMESCA, a society that covers all the non-state healthcare activities. That time it was representatives from all of the catholic and evangelic missions running clinics and smaller hospitals. There were a few dozen nurses and five doctors – two Italians, a Swede, an American and I. I don't know of any other white doctors working in the country. The girl who so warmly invites us for lunch is a nurse from Spain, a volunteer like me. She works here in Mogumba at the infirmary attached to the mission, and takes care of the leprosarium, too. She remembers me from that very meeting, because I was the only new face among the doctors. "You've picked the right day," she turns to me: "We're having a special lunch today, it's a Spanish national holiday and we're all from Spain here: My friend and me, and a married couple. We all work here as volunteers." "Wait a minute," I interrupt her, "and where then is the priest and the nuns? We're at a mission, aren't we?" The girl just sadly smiles: "There used to be nuns here, but they gradually passed away. As you know, there are less and less sisters in Europe, and there is nobody to replace them. The same thing is happening to the community of priests. There's only one left, who had to leave for Europe for a few months. Except for us, there are no other Europeans here. "And what do the natives say about that?" The Spanish girl laughs: "They still can't make heads

By the concrete pier, you can now see merely a few pirogues carved out of a single piece of trunk; they belong to local fishermen.

or tails why we, "new sisters", don't wear habits, and varnish our nails. Sometimes I even swim in the river. The "original" nuns never did things like that. So when the local children spot me in the water, they run away panic-stricken, because they take me for Mamiota, the white water nymph."

We enjoy our delicious lunch, and we enjoy ourselves, too. Jan and Joseph are excessively content at how we managed with "organizing" the trip.

I tell our new friends about the bureaucratic captain who asked us to fill out the logbook. She just shakes her head in disbelief. "So you're coming directly from Bangui? But the road through the rainforest is impassable! You're then the first ones who got here via this route since the rainy season ended!" While Joseph assures them that it was not a problem at all, I welcome the information and I am very happy one can get to Mogumba also via M'Baiki. It's about 60 miles longer, but it's kept, and it's passable. We shall have to return on this route; we can't take the chance Joseph wouldn't make it across the swamp for a second time.

After lunch, our friends take us for a stroll through the city. Mogumba used to be famous. The notorious dictator Bokassa, who ruled the country during the 1960s and 70s, was born here. He supported his hometown in various ways. He built a hospital here, and a gymnasium even. But time thwarted all of this. Only a fragment remains from the gym, and the once imposing buildings on the main street are falling apart and sprouting with shrubs. Also the formerly significant port lost all its significance. By the concrete pier, you can now see only a few pirogues carved out of a single piece of trunk; they belong to local fishermen.

Right next to the port, there is a whole neighborhood of shabby houses made of bamboo. It's a refugee camp from war torn Congo, which borders the Central African Republic right across the river. The camp left in us a terrible feeling. I have seen a great deal of African cities and villages during the past year, but never before had I been confronted with such terrible poverty and desperation like there.

Then we visit the local hospital. If for nothing else, I want to see it out of professional interest. "Follow me then, but we must be quick," our guide tries to comply, saying: "The native nurses here don't like to see me, they think I ruin their business with my small mission infirmary. I try to do my best, to find ways to help the poor people. The hospital nurses' only interest is to do the patient out of as much money as they can. The locals know this, and that's why they don't really come here." She was right. Quickly I walk through the hospital, and peep in the rooms. They are empty. There are just four patients, altogether. A small, exceedingly dehydrated newborn suffering from diarrhea is one of them. "What medication does he get?" I ask his father, who sits helplessly at the bed. He shows me a prescription for four expensive antibiotics he could afford to obtain only for a single day of treatment. He has no more money left. Now he just waits and hopes. "What an absurd treatment!" I wonder, "It merely impoverishes the family of the poor father!" "The most important thing is to replenish the liquids," I explain to the unhappy father, and I advise him to dissolve eight lumps of sugar and a teaspoon of salt in two pints of water. Then I tell him how often the little patient should use it. "This can't be possible," I look at the Spanish girl, shaking my head. "How come the local doctor allows such things?" "There's none," she shrugs her shoulders. "And what about caesarian sections, hernias, and other such basic things that must be operated? You don't operate at the clinic, do you?" "No, I don't know how," she replies sadly, "that's why so many people die here." We aren't allowed to stay at the hospital any longer.

Returning to the mission, I silently watch the beautiful tropical flora, gradually taking control of the streets of Mogumba. I can't take my eyes off of all the palm trees, blossoming hibiscuses, banana trees, and all the other plants unknown to me. As if the girl was reading my thoughts: "It looks like paradise, but living here can be hell."

There is still a long way ahead of us, and we need to be in Bangui in the evening, the only option is to hit the road again. This time via M'Baiki. This route is longer, but safer. Its well kept and goes through inhabited areas.

Yes, every moment we pass by a little village lurking under the rainforest giants. On small wooden tables the villagers exhibit their goods, offering their harvest for sale. Joseph pulls up every once in a while, haggles without compromise, and fills the body of our car with huge and weighty bunches of bananas for cooking, pineapples, various spices, etc. In short, with products which don't grow in the Bozoum region. He is looking forward to making a good profit by selling what he had bought here for a song upon our return. "Joseph, we don't have that much time left," I tell him at the next business halt. "Don't you worry, doctor," he calms me down, "we'll manage without any problems." As he starts the Mitsubishi, I think I can tell what he thinks: "I really love the rainforest. Everything is so cheap in here."

We arrive at the airport after dark. We're told the plane will arrive around midnight, but nobody knows the exact time of arrival here.

All weary we head back to the Centre d'accueil, just to take a short rest. The telephone is out of order in the accommodation center, so before midnight we walk back to the streets to obtain information about the arrival of the Paris plane. "Can't tell you anything further, try to call in two hours," the voice at the other end replies. It's clear we won't get much sleep tonight. When we try around 2am, the phone just keeps ringing. "I guess the plane is landing, and they're all busy navigating it," Joseph speculates, "they don't bother about calls then." I am on pins and needles. "Let's go to the airport!" I urge everybody. It's a real surprise when we get there. The airport building stands in darkness, and with only a few emergency lights on. Silence everywhere. "So we're here in vain," Jan laments. "There," Joseph looks into the darkness, pointing to a bright northern star. Yes, the star is drawing near. In about ten minutes, it becomes clear that it's a plane. Soon it lands on the runway, roaring. The lights turn on quickly in both the airport building and the navigation tower. Soldiers and the flight personnel are rushing headlong out of the doors. "This can't be true! They were sleeping! That's why they wouldn't pick up the phone," cries Joseph, taken by surprise. We all exchange surprised looks, and I really can't tell, whether Joseph is serious. It's virtually out of the question that a huge airliner would land in a capital city without anybody taking notice. But after a year spent in Africa, I understand anything is possible.

Jan and I push our heads in between the planks of the fence, surveying the passengers leaving the plane. There are no whites among them. "So they didn't arrive," Jan says, disappointed.

Eventually we learn with Joseph from a soldier at the entry to the passenger terminal that this very plane had departed from Benin, and that the estimated arrival of the Paris plane – the one we've been awaiting for almost two days – is sometime in the morning.

The long expected journalists actually arrive in the morning. They are full of enthusiasm, and eager to start filming straight away in the capital. Since I am aware that taking pictures and filming is prohibited here, and that it's very easy to get thrown into the Bangui prison because of it, we head for the Centre d'accueil for breakfast as soon as we get their luggage, and we set out for Bozoum right after. There they can film Africa as much as they like.

Chapter Nineteen

The Evening with Our Guests

We reach Bozoum with the sunset after a daylong exhausting drive. The journalists are already expected at the mission. Great welcomes and introductions take place.

"Let's have something to eat, you must be terribly hungry!" Marcello invites us. We all take seats at a long table. We are happy to be together again, and to have some new faces with us, too.

"When was the last time you had some visitors like us?" one journalist asks me. "Hmmm," I am trying to think, "Well, if I don't count the missionaries from neighboring stations, it must have been about eight months ago. It was in the spring, a group from Doctors without Borders spent the night here. It was when an epidemic of meningitis erupted in the area north of Bozoum. We also recorded a few deaths, but it was much less than in Boccaranga or N'Ganuday. The task of the team was to deliver antibiotics to the small villages in the infected areas, and provide help organizing the inoculation. They also left a bunch of

It was in the spring, a team of Doctors without Borders spent the night here.

packages of oil type Chloramphenicol with us. This is normally only used during an epidemic. Its main advantage is that a single dose covers the whole treatment: once injected into muscle, it gradually releases itself into the organism. The doctors can then let families take care of their sick, and move on to other stricken villages. The project was well though out, just like their other projects and the structure of the organization itself. It was a nice visit. They helped me a great deal in the hospital, and I also learned a lot of interesting things from them.

A young German woman was in charge of the team. The opportunity to talk to somebody from Europe, and moreover, from my line of work made me very happy. My German colleague couldn't understand that a European doctor could be working in the bush, in a hospital "just by himself". It was quite a surprise to her. I still remember our friendly conversation as we sat on the veranda.

"And when you fall sick, what are you going to do?" "I would ask father Marcello to drive me to the capital, it's easy to be repatriated by a plane from there." She smiled: "But it takes a whole day to travel to Bangui, and the plane to Europe flies only once a week. If you get malaria impacting your brain, or have a crash with this little car of yours, you would die on the way for sure." After her words, I took a glimpse at their big, modern Toyota Jeep. Next to it, my Citroën CV3 seemed like a mere toy. I had to ask her then: "So tell me, how have you worked this out?" "In case of life danger, a small plane would come for us anywhere. We communicate with the central office in Barcelona every evening." She pointed to the other end of the veranda, where a loud conversation was taking place. Other members of the expedition were just attaching a gadget to their notebook to communicate messages via satellite. The antenna wasn't any bigger than a small, opened book. "I can't get my message through," the Spanish doctor said. "The satellite over the Indian ocean is overloaded." "Let's then try the other one over the Atlantic," replied the Italian, turning the antenna by 180 degrees.

"Why don't you work with us?" My colleague took me by surprise, "I have a cool spot for you in Afghanistan!" I just laughed: "No, I like it here." "Good! Message sent!" A happy exclamation interrupted us. I couldn't resist sending an email to Prague. I sent a greeting to my father. Later I learned he had really wondered about the message reaching his computer at work.

"So you don't have a phone here?" The journalist interrupts my talk. "Oh no, the satellite telephones exist, of course, but they are extremely expensive. We just have a regular CB here. At a set time, twice a week, we connect to the monastery at the Italian Arenzano."

Soon our talk takes on a different direction. We plan with the journalists the schedule for tomorrow. "We would like to film the everyday life of the natives in the town," the other journalist says. "We're interested in seeing some of the surroundings around here. We'd also like to take a look in the hospital, but mainly, we would like to film a mass in one of the small villages in the bush."

We suggest Hai, where stands a primitive small church of raw brick and a hay roof.

We suggest Hai, where stands a primitive small church of raw brick and a hay roof. "The surrounding rocks are just made for filming," I suggest. "The first rocks of the Karré range rise at a 300 foot distance from the village. These are huge rocks, reminiscent more of the Ayers Rock in Australia than mountains. It'll surprise you seeing a black, sloping wall rising from a perfectly flat plain. It looks like a steep roof with its vertical distance of about 1/5 mile. It's virtually free of vegetation, and on its very peak there is a beautiful plateau with tiny pools in the dips of the rock, and with a beautiful outlook of more, and more boulders." I take a small pause before I proceed, "the real rarity are the weird trees which look like cactuses. After you break off one of the tough leaves, white juice starts dripping. The locals told me it's a virulent poison." The journalists sit up: "We can't miss such a thing!"

"Marcel, go and show them your painting," Marcello enters into the conversation. "How come you're a doctor, and you paint?" Our friends wonder. "I don't really," I object, "but one must cope with everything here in Africa."

It was about six months ago. One afternoon, I decided to go and sketch the Bozoum mission for remembrance. I sat at the little square facing the church with a pencil and a scrap of paper, and began to draw. Soon a little black boy passed by. He stopped, snoopily looking over my shoulder. It didn't take long, and there stood another. He was also very much interested in what I was doing. Soon there was a throng of about twenty little shrimps behind my back, who were snickering and pointing to the picture they were comparing with reality: "Moh bah, yangah, kekeh… – See, a door, a tree…"

Because no secret can be kept in Africa, they learned about my sketching also at the mission. "Father Norberto is just about to finish building a small chapel in the village of Boyelé. And we need a picture of St. Francis in the chapel," Marcello commented one day at dinner, "Marcel, do you think you could paint it for us?" "What? I'm not a painter." I protested. "But I've heard you know how to do it," Marcello didn't get discouraged. "Sometimes I sketch something on paper," I admitted. "Well, this time, it'd be a little bigger," the boss of the mission was coaxing me, "a painting about 3 x 7ft in size, and in colors. "That's impossible," I said, and I wouldn't talk about it any longer. Marcello, however, stayed stiff-necked. In the following weeks he kept persuading me that a new chapel asks for a new picture, and that I was the only one at the mission who could do more than paint a wall. What could I do? Norberto gave me a large piece of plywood and some cans of the oil paint used for fences and eaves. Marcello also insisted that apart from the figure of the saint, there should be a black wolf, and some nature as well.

Titus served me as a model for the wolf. Titus is our huge guard dog who wonderfully protects our mission scaring off all of the thieves and dubious individuals. The reason is that the natives have never come across a big black dog like him. They are used to the dogs living in the savanna – small and reddish. As far as "nature" was concerned, I had to make do with the hibiscus blossoms creeping up the wall. As a model for the Saint I chose

It took me almost three months to finish the picture.

Maurice, our night watchman, who had a lot of fun in the process. The evenings were the only time I had for painting, so I had to work on it piece by piece. The burning kerosene lamp would always attract all kinds of vermin and insects, including mosquitoes that were constantly gluing themselves to the drying paint. In order to proceed the next day, I had to scratch off all the insects with emery paper first, and then mend the ruined spots. It took me almost three months to finish the picture.

"The natives like it a lot," Marcello relishes. "Hmmm, that's nice," one of the two journalists nods his head, "so are there original paintings even in the scattered villages in the bush?" "Yes, of course, some of these chapels are worth a lot, you know." I laugh. "Listen, let me tell you what I heard from Enrico, one Italian volunteer who comes every year spending his vacation helping Norberto to build schools and chapels in the bush.

Enrico was building a small chapel in one village. As usual, he brought to the site sacks with cement and sand he dug up in a nearby stream. After a few weeks, the chapel was almost ready, with only the roof and some details missing, a jeep pulled up at the site. A few men armed with automatics jumped out. They looked around threateningly, pointing their guns at the native workers. Then an Arab with heavy golden rings and mirrored sunglasses got out of the car. He closely inspected the heaps of remaining sand and barked: "Where did you get the sand?" "From the river here, of course," Enrico calmly replied. "And who gave you permission? Don't you know that it's me who owns the concession for the mining of sand in all rivers of the prefecture?" The man was raging. Of course, Enrico didn't know anything, so he just kept shrugging his shoulders. The Arab finally shouted something at his men-at-arms. Straight away they ran to the remnants of sand, sieved it and carefully searched through it. In the heaps they found four black diamonds. Once more they angrily pointed their guns at Enrico, and off they went. Who knows, how many diamonds Enrico walled up in his chapel!

While we are talking with the journalists, the lights go off for ten seconds. It was a signal the generator would go off in a moment. We didn't even notice it's already half past nine. The light will last just about one more minute. Then the whole mission is going to immerse in the African darkness, joining all the other homes of Bozoum, which are lit only by kerosene lamps, or burning fires in front. Time to go to sleep.

Quickly we rise up from the table. The journalists hastily go through their luggage searching for flashlights; I light up the old kerosene lamp. "Buona notte!" Marcello waves at me. "Dobrou noc!" I say to the journalists. Sebastien says in English "Good night!" probably thinking about his native India. To Norberto's "Bon Soir!" I reply waving my hand. Then we exchange smiles with Sako, the night watchman, who passes by with a snake stick in his hand, wishing to everyone "Ala lango nzonih – Sleep well!"

170

Our mission, just like other African missions, is a place to encounter people of different nationalities, different languages and different cultures. It's quite amazing with what respect the people accept one another and collaborate together. They don't discuss tolerance; they live it.

I remain at the veranda by myself. The kerosene lamp with its yellow, flickering flame illuminates the long wooden table, lined up chairs, and the old box with a transmitter. The light is flickering about the old timberwork, attracting all kinds of night insects. I blow out the candle flame, and I move my chair to the edge of the veranda. It's a full moon again. The silver beams are reflected from the river in the valley, gently touching the roofs of Bozoum. From a distance I can hear drumbeats blending with chirping cicadas. From the huts, live coals are glowing into the night. Until recently I regarded them just as dying fires. Now they mean more, they indicate the houses of my friends. I am picturing their faces, their happy and less happy fortunes. I am sorry my stay is slowly ending. I like it here.

Chapter Twenty

Bozoum Prison

The next morning I hurry to the hospital again. My colleague is looking out for me in front of the pediatrics ward. It isn't doctor Baté. He managed to obtain a well-paid official job in the neighboring town, and left the hospital. A fresh graduate from the medical faculty of Bangui University, doctor Mathurin Youfegan, replaced him. This young and intelligent African likes doing things well. He is wonderful to collaborate with. It's obvious that the fate of the hospital and good management mean quite a lot to him.

"Marcel," he calls, "I have about twenty patients scheduled for ultrasound examinations this morning. Are you coming?" "Yes, definitely. Just wait for me, I need to do two minor operations before that."

Within the course of my work in the hospital, I would gradually shift my priorities. In the first months, I put all of my energy into the everyday medical practice, but later I realized it would bring more of a benefit to the locals if I try to pass my knowledge and experience gained in Europe to my Central African colleagues and collaborators. So apart from being a doctor, I was teaching as well. That way at least something would remain after me in Africa for good. One of my tasks is to teach Mathurin usage of the ultrasound. He is making progress. I will leave my French textbook here when I go.

Two medical students came to the hospital with Mathurin. In the beginning they assisted, then as they progressed I would allow them to do such minor things as sewing stitches, and now they have begun to operate with me. They are both very able, Marmoz especially. He is interested in everything, which makes me happy. We are a good team. Every day there's lots of work. Word got out that I will be leaving soon, and there's been a response to it.

Lots of people of the region are coming to the hospital to be operated on by the "white doctor". They come from Bozoum and Boccaranga, but also from Carnot hundreds of miles away, and even from the capital city. Wealthy patients mean a financial contribution for the hospital, and the poor come also, knowing I wouldn't reject them.

Because the interest is so large, I had to get a planner to enter the names of the appointed patients. All terms until my departure are full. Although I made the decision to operate until the very last day, I can't satisfy all the patients. I would love to, but I can't manage any more operations before I go. That's fine though. The Bozoum Hospital has a good reputation and doctor Mathurin will stay.

I walk to the surgical ward, and Goum asks: "Do you have some extra bandages? I need bandaging for this prisoner." I look at the forty-year-old man with a large ulcer on his leg. "Yes," I nod. I am familiar with the Bozoum prison service. It's not the first time that a prisoner came here for treatment. They always came without escort. It always seemed strange to me, so I went to have a look there sometime ago.

I went to have a look at the prison sometime ago.

The prison is at the edge of town. It consists of a few ground houses and a huge wall with glass shards on top surrounds it. Only one of the houses still maintains a hay roof. The very walls of the other houses are in ruin with the sky instead of a roof. The prisoners' environment is truly terrible. They have virtually nothing, no shelter, no food. They have a quite unusual approach there in order to keep the prisoners from dying of hunger.

It was a real surprise for me to learn the convicts stay at prison only for the night. If you expected tough guards, you would be disappointed. In the morning they always open the prison gate, so that each prisoner could go – on his own and without escort – to earn a living. Some work honestly and earn enough for food, some find other ways, their ways. One must eat. What I find really interesting is that everybody returns in the evening. I can't grasp why they simply don't run away. I can't imagine such an approach working back home. All cells would be empty from the very first night. One thing is for sure, however, their homes are often far away; the convicts are torn away from their families that may have possibly given them help. I hand a few bandages to Goum.

I have another memory of the Bozoum prison. During my visit there I got acquainted with a prison guard. He had a child shortly after, and came to the mission to ask me to be the godfather of his son he decided to name after me. Such a request cannot be

He came to the mission to ask me to be the godfather of his son he decided to name after me.

declined – it was a great honor. Central Africans usually choose godfathers only from their families.

When the boy was about two weeks old, father Marcello christened him at the mission. The ceremony was simple, but beautiful and celebratory. But that's not how the story ends. The very same day I was called to the hospital to examine a sick child. I was so surprised when I recognized my little Marcel! He cried and cried, and couldn't be eased. I found out he suffered from a strangulated hernia, that couldn't be made right. The only solution was an immediate operation, but never before was such a little child operated on here, and I myself had never performed one. How are we to put it to sleep, lest we harm it with adult medication?

Neither of my assistants Goum and Albert, nor my African colleague would have anything to do with the operation. They sensed it could end up badly, and they feared the consequences. The father suggested he would rent a car and drive the child to the capital in the morning, but that could be too late. The desperate mother was merely clutching the child to her chest, not daring to enter the conversation of men.

I was by no means eager to operate. It was definitely a very risky enterprise, operating on a newborn should be embarked upon only by an experienced child surgeon, and I certainly am not. Moreover, the life of my godchild was at stake! I became his godfather in the afternoon, was he now to die at my operation table? I could have resigned and let the boy die in his family circle, and no one in the hospital would blame me. The child would die at home. However, once we decide to operate and the child doesn't survive, I, and my colleagues will face great difficulties. I took advantage of my authority and talked others into rolling the dice on it. I was determined to gamble.

First of all, we firmly strapped up the baby so it wouldn't wiggle around, injected hypnotics in his bottom, and then I deadened the area in question with local anesthetic. Of course, this primitive method is not used in Europe any longer, but it came in handy to me. Although I didn't have magnifying glasses and the cut itself wasn't bigger than adult's nail, the operation turned out well. I was very happy about it. It was the best christening present I could give to little Marcel. Later I realized, how lucky I was. For a couple of months after that, before the prison guard's family moved to Bangui, the thankful mother brought the child to the hospital, to show me how healthily he was growing.

I finish my work in the operating room before midday, and join Mathurin, who has started examining already. The little ultrasound is the most hi-tech gadget in our hospital. Not only in our hospital. There is no such instrument for hundreds of miles around. It provides us with valuable information especially during the gynecological and pre-birth examinations. It's very popular among the natives, especially the Bozoum women. Some of them even believe it cures infertility.

Mathurin uses ultrasound today within the framework of his gynecological consultations. He is brilliant. Just when I enter into the room, I hear him concluding his examination saying to a young woman: "Don't worry, you're not sick, you are going to have a baby!" The woman beams after hearing the positive news. Children are always welcomed in Africa. "Talk to the birth assistant, Regina, she's going to give you regular examinations during your pregnancy." This is an absolute rarity! The vast majority of future mothers never come for pre-birth check ups, and just a few give birth in a hospital. This woman comes from a wealthier family, so she can afford preventive care.

"Marcel," Mathurin points at another patient, "I cured this woman for a gynecological infection about a month ago. She's sick again." "Did your husband undergo the treatment, too?" "Yes," she replies shortly. "Hmmm, then the treatment should take effect," I keep thinking. Suddenly I realized: "And your husband, does he have other wives?" She nods quietly: "Yes, three more." "Well, this won't work," Mathurin shakes his head, rebuking her: "It makes no sense to prescribe anything to you. If you want to get cured, talk first to your husband and the other wives, and then come with the whole family." When the patient left, I asked my colleague: "Is she going to return?" "I don't know," Mathurin shrugs his shoulders. "Men here do whatever they feel like." He is right about that. I learned about it, too.

I remember a patient with a similar kind of disease I examined some time ago. I prescribed antibiotics to her and her husband. The patient appeared soon in the hospital again, showing the same symptoms as before. Finally she confessed that her husband had rolled a cigarette from my prescription, and then smoked it with great gusto.

At the close of the exhausting day, spent mostly in the operating room, I go and check on the rebinding of one little boy. It's a particularly interesting case. He stumbled into a fire some years ago, and badly burnt his hand. Over the course of the years, the burns healed, but rigid scars hindered his fingers from motion. The scars had to be cut off, and the skin replaced, but I am not a plastic surgeon, and had no clue how. Then I recalled I had met one doctor, a specialist in hand surgery, during my stay in Lyon. I found his address in my notebook, and sent him a fax via Mr. Buhl. I informed him about the boy's complaint, asking for advice. I don't know whether he still remembered me, but he replied straight away. Precisely, step-by-step, he described how to proceed during the operation. Thanks to the willingness of the doctor to offer us this help, I was able to operate successfully on the little boy.

Chapter Twenty-One

My Last Days in Africa

I clutch convulsively to the side of the car as it bucks up like a stampeded horse. Every moment I flutter into the air to fall back to the wooden bench; I keep knocking myself on it. Sitting is just impossible. I prefer to hold on tight to the frame, and with my legs bent at the knees I muffle the constant bumps. It's really exhausting. After a few-hour-drive, my legs will be like after a day of downhill skiing.

My cloth hat protects me dependably from the direct sunlight. I don't even feel the heat during the fast ride. Still, this doesn't make its beams less dangerous. What I mind, however, are the clouds of red dust towering behind the car and the small insects, which keep repeatedly getting into my eyes and nose. That's why I covered my nose and mouth with a bandana, and I protect my eyes with sunglasses, fastened with a string at my nape.

We are on the road for thirty minutes. We are just passing the last huts at the edge of Bouar. We're in a rush. My colleagues from the hospital prepared a goodbye party for me this evening. I can't wait to get there. It's still a long way to go, however. If everything goes well, I estimate about three more hours of this shattering drive.

I am hopping from side to side, hardly keeping balance, and then there comes a strong blow. Marcello brakes fiercely. Inertia makes me hit the backside of the cabin. "What happened?" I call out to the driver. But Marcello is getting out of the car already. Quickly I jump down. "We blew a tire," he says with poise. Clouds of whirling dust slowly subside. "That's a fine kettle of fish," I think morosely, "this means a further delay." Marcello understands, he isn't happy about it either. Quickly we get down to change the wheel. After thirty minutes, we turn around, and head back to Bouar. "That's the only thing we can do," Marcello says apologetically, "but I won't set off into the bush without a spare, it'd be sheer madness."

I am silent and uneasy. "It was quite a delay with the change of the wheel, and now we are returning to get the hole patched. Moreover, darkness falls when we're still on the way to Bozoum, and makes us drive even more slowly. There is no chance of arriving to the party in time. Rotten luck! I won't be able to say a nice goodbye to my colleagues after the year we spent working together."

The Main Street of Bouar, formerly the second most important city of the Central African Republic, is just a clay road, hemmed by one-story grocery shops. Its assortment isn't any different from the goods offered in Bozoum. It's chiefly groceries and textiles imported from neighboring Cameroon. Gone are the days when there was a regular line between Bangui and Paris, when the city was famous for its nightlife! Since 1998, when the last French soldiers left, the city is as if under a spell. No planes land here, the hospital doesn't really function, there are no factories, and the city has turned into one large village.

We arrive at the service station. At the verge of the dusty road there sits a young African next to a heap of old tires and a barrow with a gas compressor. We take out the flat tire. The boy readily launches into his work. First he loosens the tire with a lever, takes the tube out, and cleanses the verges of the rupture with a flat stone. He cuts off an appropriate piece from an old tire, and brushes it strenuously with the stone until it's all clean. Then he conjures up a smeared jar with glue, patches the rupture, and weights it down. After a while, he inflates the tire with the compressor, and plunges it into a washbowl to assure us the air doesn't leak. We are content. We place the spare back in the car and set out for Bozoum for the second time today.

The shadows are growing longer. We have lost about two hours by now. The delay will be much longer, however. I am sure about that.

Yes. Because of the difficult night ride, we reach Bozoum after a three-hour delay. My pessimistic assumption was met. I entertain no hopes today's party will take place.

Straight away after our arrival I head to the hospital to make apologies. When I pull up at the grounds, the nurse on duty runs up to me. "Great you're here, doctor! Go right away to the restaurant Côte d'Azure. Everyone is expecting you." This assurance makes me breathless. I really hadn't expected this.

The restaurant is at the edge of town. It's a small, one-story house with a little backyard, fenced with hay matting. The only drinks to order are bottled beer imported from the capital and coke from Cameroon. You need to bring your own food.

The street lamps are again out of order. I pull up at the small, dark yard and switch off the engine and the lights. I go inside. Darkness everywhere. As my eyes finally get used to the dark, I discern plenty of people sitting around a long table underneath the night sky. I find out everyone is there: Mathurin, Albert, Goum, Semplice, Regine, Jean-Paul and many others. I am stunned and moved. These people had no idea of what had happened to us, yet they have been patiently waiting for me in the dark. For two hours at least! Nobody would start eating until I arrived.

The only light emerges from a burning candle on the floor by the table. A nurse from the pediatrics ward slowly dances around it. "Bonsoir, mon docteur – Good evening, doctor!" he greets me with an austere expression, "I have been expecting you from half past two." Mathurin bursts out with laughter: "He's just saying, he personally began the party right after lunch, and as you can see, he was starting to get a tad thirsty." We all laugh.

Mathurin then asks that the kerosene lamps be lighted, and the traditional homemade food be brought to the table. We enjoy vegetable salads with traditional manioc of chicken and goat meat. We wash it down with Central African beer "33". We talk with animation, evoking the joyful and less happy stories we went through together during our year together in the hospital. "If the locals knew when exactly you were leaving, they'd definitely stop you," one of the invited officials tells me.

After dinner one colleague brings along a tape player with batteries. We all enjoy ourselves. We dance to the rhythms of African music until midnight. The party turned out nicely. It was a beautiful, unforgettable evening.

In the next days, banquets awaited me also at the mission and at the parish. These were just as nice and friendly as the evening with my colleagues from the hospital.

It's the evening before my departure. I went through my things during the day. There isn't much left. Much of my clothing I gave to those who might need it, since I certainly won't be lacking it in Europe. Managing the storage of the medicine at the mission took a lot more time. I left medical material which sisters Marie-René and Christiane might use in their infirmary, and the rest I consigned to Albert and Goum. They will make use of it when helping the poorer inhabitants.

It's getting dark. I take my last stroll along the houses of Bozoum. People run out of their huts to say goodbye and they have tears in their eyes. I drop by at a few friends'. We sit for a while at their fireplaces, and we shake hand for the last time. The old "Baba" Jacques, who had undergone two hernia operations, insists on giving me some kind of goodbye present. Finally he picks up a nice specimen of pumpkin from his field. A huge one, the size of one third of my suitcase. I can't decline. I gratefully accept the gift, but eventually I leave it at the mission, it's too big and much too heavy for plane transportation.

I planned a short walk, but I return late at night. It made me sad saying goodbye to all these people. I took a liking to Bozoum in these twelve months.

Early in the morning I climb to the Binot hill. From its peak I watch the morning sun melting down the mist of the valley. I look at the hay roofs of the houses, the green fields and the bluish rocks of the Karré range in the horizon. I promise myself I will come back one day.

Straight after breakfast I get ready for the journey. I put my luggage in the back of Marcello's car, saying goodbye to all the people I spent one year with – the Carmelite fathers, and sisters from the neighborhood, the cook, the watchmen, our dog Titus and many other people at the gate. Last hugs, last handshakes and wishes of a nice journey. I am moved.

Time runs mercilessly! The sun is growing strong. "Doctor, in order to avoid the midday heat at least for a part of the trip, we need to go!" Joseph waves at me, restlessly. He's waiting at the loaded van. He's right. It's time to go. Jan and the two journalists get into the car, too. Although they booked a different plane, we leave together from here. Albert gets in the car, too. He would insist on seeing me out, on behalf of the hospital, to my very plane. Finally we hit the road. I am looking out the window, waving until the mission gate disappears at the curve.

Chapter Twenty-Two

Coming Home

I have fallen in love with Africa, but still I can't wait to be back home. In the Bangui airport I meet Angelo, the dentist, once again; he came here from the Yolé mission. "Together we came, together we part!" He greets me from a distance, adding: "I am really looking forward to some cooler air. As usual, I am going to spend Christmas with my relatives in Italy."

Although our plane leaves tomorrow, we must check in our luggage at the Air France office today. We go there together in the afternoon.

The heat is terrible. The line proceeds at a desperately slow pace. The customs officer has been grubbing through the personal belongings of an Indian standing before me; the scrutiny is still not over. "Oh, aren't they just lovely!" She takes a pair of sunglasses out of his suitcase, and surveys them closely, taking a fancy to them. "You can keep them," the Indian man finally submits. His inspection is over. Now it's our turn. "É sempre così – It's always like this," he remarks in Italian, so the clerk wouldn't understand.

The baggage check runs smoothly beyond expectation. Neither of us actually has much in our suitcases. Angelo, who is returning back to Africa after the four-week vacation, left almost all his stuff up in Yolé; I gave most of my things away.

Just as we reach the Centre d'accueil, darkness falls on the city. My last hot and humid tropical night begins.

Before dinner, I settle myself into an armchair on the veranda, and listen to the singing of the well-known African choir, which is rehearsing for tomorrow's Holy Mass. I understand every word they sing. Only the yard wall separates us. I recall the moment when I was sitting here one year ago. Then I thought I would be giving something to Africa, but now – twelve months later – it seems different. I guess I am bringing back much more than I "gave".

The one-year sojourn in the bush has definitely enriched my professional life, and brought me a great deal of medical experience. Mainly, however, it's been a good growing experience. In the poor local conditions, where nothing is self-evident, it's much clearer to see what is really substantial, and what is not. There are only a few substantial values. The ones attacking us persistently from TV commercials are not substantial.

I know the songs in Sango that are now reaching my ears. I would often hear them in Bozoum. In the voices of the native singers, there mingles the joy and sadness of the sensitive African soul. Suddenly I realize that Africa is actually saying goodbye now, there won't be time for this tomorrow. The silver moon slowly climbs the sky.

We get up early the next day. We have a quick breakfast, and then we set out for the airport to be there as early as possible. There are a number of inspections awaiting us.

As we are walking past the soldiers who guard the passenger terminal, I turn to wave to my good friends, Joseph, Albert and Jan, who accompanied me for hundreds of miles.

A policewoman at the counter hesitates before she gives me the passport stamp: "It's Christmas, and my children are at home waiting for presents." She says, in a by-the-way manner. "Nginzah ah yekeh apeh – No money," I remain unshaken, knowing that local customs officers aren't poor at all. I am also not lying. All I have is a few coins in my pocket to telephone my parents from Paris. I know they wont to come to the airport. The policewomen frowns, but I get my stamp.

Nothing can stop me now from boarding the plane, and taking that step into the other world I had left a year ago. All I must do is cross the threshold.

The plane takes off slowly. Gradually it gains speed and leaps off. One more wobble, and we rise steeply. The airport building soon disappears from sight. I look out of the window, saying goodbye to the places that grew so close to me, where I spent one beautiful and unforgettable year of my life.

Our flight to Paris goes by very quickly. Alternately, Angelo and I doze, talk a bit, or have something to eat, and watch the fascinating countryside below: the swamps around Chad Lake, the never ending desert sands of the Erg, the huge black rocks of the mythical Range of Tibesti, the Mediterranean coasts of Libya and Tunis. When we are flying above Marseille, I already feel half home. Soon we land at the Charles de Gaul International Airport in Paris. I walk into the harsh, wet coldness. With nostalgia I recall the blazing African sun.

Angelo carries on to Milan, I take the ÈSA line to Prague. "Klidnì mluvte èesky, já rozumím – Feel free to speak in Czech, I understand," I tell the flight attendant who had welcomed me in French on board our plane. She looks at me distrustfully. Sunburn, wearing a straw hat, with an Arabic mat in my hand – I somehow don't fit in the company of the polished businessmen with their suitcases.

Beams of winter sun break through the rarefied clouds above Prague. We are landing. I can recognize Dejvice, Bohnice, Prague Castle... The cabin resounds with tones of Smetana's Vltava. I hear Czech spoken around me, and I am happy to be back home. After a long time I embrace my parents and siblings. We are all happy. I know that in a few days, everything will return back to normal, and that eventually, my African adventure will seem to me like a dream. Still, I know at the same time I won't forget Africa until I die.

"Marcel," sister Marina once told me, when we were returning from some Bozoum neighborhood back to the mission, "I really like the stars here in Africa. They seem somehow bigger and brighter than in Italy or in Uruguay back home." Now I know she was right. In Africa, the heaven really is nearer to the earth.

Epilogue

More than two years have passed since my arrival from Africa. During this period I have tried to share my experience with the greater public. I went through various meetings and lectures in Prague, as well as other places in the Czech Republic. Keen interest and the willingness – especially of the younger people – in helping the people of the poor country made me very happy.

It's a pity, however, there are virtually no programs in the Czech Republic – as common as they are in the western world – that would make it possible to transform all of this good will into concrete projects. But I am sure this is going to change soon.

I've returned to Africa twice since then. Both were short-term visits: I informed young African doctors in Bozoum and N'Ganuday about elementary methods in child surgery, since the field is in its absolute beginnings in the Central African Republic.

I also became involved in the interesting project of the Carmelite Order to build a smaller, well-equipped hospital near Bouar.

In October 2002, after an ineffectual coup d'état organized by general Bozizé, the whole country bogged down in the chaos of civil war. The intricate political situation led to another – this time successful – takeover in 2003. The country changed its government and president.

The months long fights struck Bozoum in January 2003, bringing an end to both the mission and the hospital, and causing the suffering and death of many inhabitants. A large number of other cities, especially in the northern part, have been affected in the same way. The country is now once again slowly recovering. Despite all the hardship and suffering, the village people keep working in their fields, and the missions in Baoro and Bouar, though under difficult conditions, still exist. In August 2003 the renewal of the Bozoum mission and hospital was started. Central Africa thus doesn't lose its cruelly tested hope.

I recall the lyrics of a song, my Central African friends had sung to me: "Fini la a sigigi, Africa lo londo... A new day comes and Africa arises..." I really hope for this to happen.

Prague, September 2003

Marcel Drlík, M.D.

Central African Republic

Number of inhabitants: 3.04 million (1990)
Area: 622,436 sq. km =243,139 sq. miles
Capital City: Bangui
History: The target of slave raids since the 17th century. 1894–1946 French colony (Oubangui – Shari). 1946–1958 French Overseas Zone. 1960 declares independence. In 1966 military coup d'état, with the dictator Bocassa as the head of the state. 1976–1979 Became imperial regime. In 1979 Bocassa

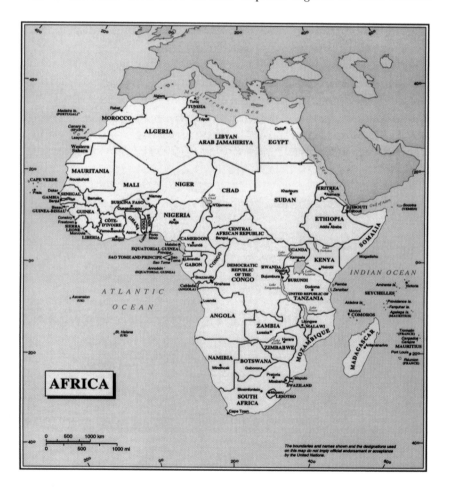

overthrown and the Republic renewed. 1981-1985 military regime, then civil regime again. In 2003 coup d'état.

Climate: Tropical, humid, equatorial. Tropical vegetation, equatorial and gallerian forests and tall-grassy plants.

Economy: Underdeveloped country dependant on the exploitation of mineral resources and timber.

For informations:
O. Anastasio Roggero, OCD
PROKURA KARMELITÁNSKÝCH MISIÍ
KLÁŠTER PRAŽSKÉHO JEZULÁTKA
Karmelitská 9, 118 00 Praha 1
Phone: 00420 257 533 646
Fax: 00420 257 530 370
E-mail: mail@pragjesu.info
www.pragjesu.info

To send offerings please
use the following:
Name of the account:
Klášter Pražského Jezulátka
Swift code: BACXCZPP
Account n.:
CZ9327000000006024090001
HVB Bank Czech Republic a.s.
Nám. Republiky 3a
110 05 Praha 1, POB 48
Czech Republic

CZECH DOCTOR IN THE HEART OF AFRICA

Text by Marcel Drlík, M.D.
Translated from Czech by Ondřej Skovajsa
Edited by Ilya Kadrevis
Illustrations by Marcel Drlík, M.D.
Photographs by Marcel Drlík, M.D.
Graphic design by Tomáš Ritter

Designed and produced by AVENTINUM, s.r.o.
Tolstého 22, 101 00 Prague 10, Czech Republic
Printed in Slovakia by Magnus Press a.s.

www.aventinum.cz

ISBN 80-86858-16-2